EMERGENCY PLANNING IN IRELAND

Patrick A. O'Riordan

Institute of Public Administration

First published 1992
Institute of Public Administration
57-61 Lansdowne Road
Dublin 4
Ireland

ISBN 1 872002 56 0

British Library Cataloguing-in-Publication Data

A catalogue record for this book is available
from the British Library.

Cover, depicting the distress signal SOS in semaphore, designed by
Butler Claffey Design, Dún Laoghaire
Typeset in 11/12 Baskerville by Phototype-Set Ltd., Dublin
Printed by Colour Books, Dublin

Contents

Acknowledgements

This work is based on a thesis which was submitted to the University of Limerick in August 1991. Information and assistance was received from many sources during its preparation and I would like to acknowledge in particular the help and co-operation of Mr D. Doherty, Chief Executive Officer Mid-Western Health Board, who suggested emergency planning as a topic for research and subsequently encouraged this publication; Dr E. McCann of the University of Limerick who provided valuable guidance during the preparation of the thesis; Capt B. Phelan, Chief Ambulance Officer Southern Health Board, who made his considerable knowledge of this subject available at all times; Mr P. Robinson, Deputy Chief Executive Officer Mid-Western Health Board, who provided a valuable insight into the local planning process; Mr F. Ahern, Principal Officer, Department of Health and Mr J. Barry, Assistant Fire Advisor, Department of the Environment, who provided many helpful suggestions and information.

Finally I would like to express particular gratitude to my wife Bríd and children Sorcha, Triona and Aisling for their unwavering encouragement and support.

Patrick A. O'Riordan

April 1992

Introduction

At 6.25 p.m. on Wednesday, 21 December 1988, a Pan
American Boeing 747 took off from Heathrow Airport
bound for New York as Flight 103. At 7.03 p.m. a terrorist
device exploded in the forward cargo hold and the aircraft
crashed onto Lockerbie, a small market town of 3,500
inhabitants in the south-west of Scotland, killing all 259
persons on board. Substantial sections of the aircraft fell at
four separate locations within the town, causing explosions
and starting fires which killed eleven local people and
destroyed a number of buildings. Other wreckage, bodies
and debris were strewn over a wide area in and around
Lockerbie.

Within minutes of the crash the police and fire brigade
services of Dumfries and Galloway Regional Council were
notified and when the extent of the disaster became
apparent the council's Major Incident Plan was activated.[1]
By 10.30 p.m. there were thirty-six ambulances and a mobile
ambulance control unit in the town, and the search for
survivors and later for bodies continued throughout the
night. More than one thousand police were drafted into the
town to take part in the search for victims, control traffic,
maintain law and order and begin an investigation of the
incident. Fire brigade units from local and neighbouring
districts were mobilised and twenty units fought the various
fires that had erupted in different areas of the town.

Within an hour of the incident an Emergency Control
Centre had been established at the headquarters of the council
and this centre was transferred to Lockerbie the following
morning. From the outset council staff at the centre were
involved in the control and co-ordination of the emergency
work, the provision of assistance to survivors and evacuees,
and the provision of food and shelter for emergency service

1

personnel. Arrangements were made to comfort the bereaved relatives of passengers and crew arriving in the town as well as bereaved locals. Temporary accommodation was provided for people whose homes had been destroyed or damaged. Intensive support was provided to the local community, including the provision of money, clothing and other essentials to those in urgent need. Eventually, damaged buildings and services were repaired, restored and rebuilt as necessary.

The council estimates that more than one thousand media representatives visited Lockerbie in the immediate aftermath of the crash and as a result the local telephone exchange was quickly overloaded and all available mobile telephone channels were occupied. Council staff organised a press office to facilitate the media, which was staffed on a continuous basis throughout the incident. A local school, which was closed for the holidays, was opened to provide accommodation for the media, as well as the large number of organisations which became involved in the response, including Pan Am, the FBI and the American Embassy. All of these tasks were organised and directed by council staff, who also maintained a record of all events that occurred during the response, made arrangements for the visits of dignitaries, maintained a list of all those who assisted in the response, and replied to the more than 700 messages and offers of assistance received during the disaster and its aftermath.

This extensive response, from the immediate rescue to the rebuilding, was carried out in accordance with pre-existing plans; the preparation of such plans is part of the process known as 'emergency planning'. Without such plans the council would still have organised a response but the existence of plans reduced confusion about responsibilities and ensured that the mobilisation of resources was faster and more effective than it would otherwise have been.

The emergency planning with which this study is concerned is a process by which local public sector organisations prepare for possible disasters. At its most comprehensive it consists of:

1. an analysis of the hazards facing a community and the elimination of any hazards or the mitigation of their consequences where this is feasible;
2. an analysis of the resources, physical, human and organisational, available to cope with potential disasters; and

3. planning so that these resources will be used to best effect in the response to, and recovery from, any disaster.

Emergency planning therefore is not primarily concerned with the acquisition of extra resources but involves the anticipation of problems and the projection of possible solutions within existing constraints. After the analysis of hazards and resources, basic elements include the identification of necessary post-disaster tasks, the allocation of these tasks to organisations and individuals and, most importantly, the co-ordination of the planning efforts of all potential responding groups and organisations so that the eventual response, when it is required, is co-ordinated and effective.
Since the cause, timing, location and extent of future disasters is unknown, emergency planning is, of necessity, a difficult and complex task and the existence of emergency plans does not of itself guarantee an adequate response to a disaster. Dumfries and Galloway Regional Council has a permanent Emergency Planning Department staffed by full-time trained emergency planners. In spite of that fact the deputy chief executive officer of the council, Mr W. Alexander, told a seminar in Cork on 7 September 1990 that the council's Major Incident Plan would have to be extensively revised in light of actual experiences during the disaster. This view is echoed in the report on a survey of emergency planning by the International City Management Association which concluded that: 'Local governments continue to be surprised when the standard procedures in their lengthy plans prove irrelevant in the real disaster'.[2]
The Lockerbie disaster resulted from an unfortunate chain of events which culminated in the disintegration of the aircraft over the town. However, with different weather conditions the disaster might well have occurred over Ireland. All transatlantic flights follow defined 'tracks' that are chosen primarily to minimise the cost of fuel. On 21 December 1988 the weather pattern over the Atlantic was such that the optimum route for a westward bound transatlantic flight from Heathrow was initially north-west towards Scotland. On many days of the year, however, the optimum route for such a flight is west over Ireland towards Shannon. Thus a different weather pattern on the day could have brought Flight 103 over Ireland and ultimately, perhaps, caused the subsequent disaster to occur somewhere over the Republic.

In anticipation of such an event emergency planning has been organised in Ireland under the title of major emergency planning. Like many other areas of the public service, however, the resources that have been committed to emergency planning in Ireland are small compared with the equivalent resources in Britain. Furthermore there are a number of features of local authority administration in the Republic of Ireland which are quite different from those in Britain and which have a significant bearing on emergency planning. In Britain local authorities are organised into regional councils, which are much larger than the Irish local authorities and which are responsible for a wide range of services including the fire brigades and the police. In Ireland the fire brigades are part of the local authority service, the ambulance services (outside of Dublin) are controlled by the health boards and the Garda Síochána is an independent national service. As a result, Ireland has fifty-eight major emergency plans, one for each of the thirty-one local authorities, eight health boards and eighteen Garda divisions and one for the five Garda divisions in Dublin. All of these plans are based on a model plan, which was issued by an interdepartmental committee in the early 1980s. It is intended that in the event of a disaster anywhere in the country at least three of these plans should be activated, i.e. one local authority plan, one health board plan and one Garda plan. However, unlike Britain, there is no emergency planning department in any Irish local authority or health board.

At government level responsibility for emergency planning in Britain has been allocated to the Home Office while in Ireland responsibility is spread between the Departments of the Environment, Justice and Health, with each department responsible for its own service only. At present the Department of the Environment is regarded as the 'lead' department but no department has overall responsibility for the co-ordination of the emergency planning process at local level. Furthermore, it appears there is no official in any of these departments working exclusively on emergency planning.

Emergency planning in Ireland is also complicated by organisational differences between the Garda Síochána and the two other front-line services. Local authorities and health boards are local statutory bodies with a wide range of responsibilities outside of the emergency area and with similar management structures. The Garda Síochána on the other hand is a uniformed national service with a distinct culture and a very different management structure. Thus coordination of the planning process at local level is inevitably difficult. This difficulty is exacerbated by the need for security in Garda emergency planning due to the inclusion of a number of sensitive issues. These include preparations for possible terrorist activity by subversives, precautions against lawlessness in the aftermath of a disaster and preparations for major criminal investigations. (Because of this security element, the survey of emergency planning practices in Chapter 4 is confined to local authorities and health boards.)

Despite these limitations on emergency planning in Ireland successive governments have appeared to be satisfied with the existing situation. There has been no public debate on the adequacy or otherwise of existing emergency planning, and the subject does not appear to feature on the political agenda either at local or national level.

–1–
Development of Emergency Planning

Disasters

Since earliest times human beings have suffered the effects of many different kinds of disasters. Such events are recorded at all stages of human history including the Great Flood of the Bible, the Black Death of the Middle Ages, the seventeenth-century Great Fire of London and the Irish Potato Famine of the 1840s. For many centuries these events were perceived as punishment by the gods for the sins of mankind and the word disaster is in fact based on the Latin word *astrum*, a star, reflecting the belief that the causes of disasters were to be found in the heavens.

With the passage of time a more rational approach to these events emerged as people and governments began to see that human actions often contributed, at least in part, to the death and destruction caused by disasters. This realisation led to a study of the means by which disasters could be prevented or, in cases where that was not possible, the means by which the worst effects of disasters could be ameliorated. This was the beginning of emergency planning as it is known today. An early example of such planning occurred after the Great Fire of London when building codes and fire insurance were introduced. Building codes helped to prevent the occurrence of catastrophic fires and fire insurance compensated the victims of those incidents that did occur. Today these two basic precautions still provide protection against disasters, one by mitigation and the other as an aid to recovery.

A series of internationally publicised incidents, including Three Mile Island, Chernobyl, Seveso and Bhopal, as well as local incidents in many individual countries have generated concern in much of the developed world in recent years with a perceived increase in the number and severity of disasters. This concern has been exacerbated by a growing unease at the unknown horrors which might be unleashed by a major chemical or nuclear disaster. At the same time developments in advanced technologies of all kinds, including communications and medicine, have fostered a view among the public in developed countries that the relevant authorities will be able to take action in many situations which might previously have been regarded as hopeless. In many countries these factors have combined to promote and advance the consideration of emergency planning.

International Response

The United Nations has been involved in disaster planning for many years through UNDRO, the United Nations Disaster Relief Organisation. In 1986 the UN launched a programme called APELL, Awaredness and Preparedness for Emergencies at Local Level, designed to help establish emergency planning in member countries. The UN has followed up on this development by designating the 1990s as the United Nations Decade on Disasters.

Following severe pollution of the Rhine by the Sandoz chemical spill, the European Community adopted a resolution in May 1987 setting out the Community approach to emergency planning with particular reference to co-operation between member states in the event of transnational incidents.

Increased concern with emergency planning has been reflected in many countries in legislation, including the Emergency Preparedness Act (1988) in Canada, the Civil Protection in Peacetime Act (1986) in the United Kingdom and the Disaster Act (1985) in Holland. The Republic of Ireland has no legislation on emergency planning.

Recent years have also seen a growing interest worldwide in disaster research among academics. For many years disaster research was confined to a small number of American universities, with particular emphasis by geographers on the features of regions at risk and by sociologists on the reactions of victims. Today academics in institutions as diverse as the Asian Institute of Technology in Bangkok and the University of Leiden in Holland are involved in different aspects of disaster research. In this part of the

world, one of the more notable of these institutions is the
University of Bradford where a Disaster Prevention and
Limitation Unit was established in 1988, largely in response
to the Bradford City Football Stadium fire. To date this unit
has conducted research on the frequency of disasters,
compiled a bibliographic guide to disasters and organised
annual conferences on emergency planning. The author is
not aware of any Irish academic institution where work on
disaster research or emergency planning has been initiated.

Difficulties of Promotion

The past decade has seen the introduction or extension of
formal emergency planning in many developed countries
around the world. In most countries the process has been
slow and there are very few countries where emergency
planning is fully developed. This situation is understandable
given the inherent difficulties involved for public sector
organisations in the process of emergency planning. In
general public organisations are provided with funds, raised
by taxation, to produce defined measurable outputs. For the
most part the results of emergency planning are intangibles
which do not lend themselves to measurement. This creates
problems for the traditional form of public administration
with its heavy emphasis on accounting for expenditure.

Furthermore, (in the absence of disasters or strongly
perceived threats of disasters, there is little or no public or
political pressure for emergency planning. There is also the
basic human tendency which seeks to avoid or at least delay
consideration of issues that have strong overtones of death
and suffering. Finally there is a paradox at the heart of all
emergency planning concerning the different attitudes of
local communities and national governments. From the
perspective of governments, particularly those of larger
countries, disasters appear to occur with a certain regularity
and thus the need for emergency planning is obvious. For
most local communities, on the other hand, disasters are
remote possibilities which cannot realistically compete for
attention with everyday pressing problems. When disasters
strike, however, it is local communities and the organisations within them that must deal directly with the
immediate effects. As a result there is a tendency for
initiatives on emergency planning to begin at government

level and for most promotion of emergency planning to be from the top down)

A reasonable level of interest by governments, however, does not guarantee effective emergency planning at local level. There are problems of definition on the part of governments and of conception on the part of local organisations. These problems are reflected in the interchangeable use of such words as calamity, disaster, catastrophe and major emergency. Interestingly the word emergency is usually used to describe the planning process, for example emergency management in the United States, civil emergency planning in Britain and major emergency planning in Ireland. Yet whenever an incident occurs it is almost always referred to as a disaster, for example the Kegworth disaster, the Aberfan disaster and the Stardust disaster.

This differing use of words could be accidental but most likely it reflects the difficulties most governments experience in acknowledging the inevitability of disasters within their jurisdiction. Another factor is that in most countries emergency planning began as an offshoot of the 'normal' emergency services. For the purpose of clarity this study refers to the incidents which require a response as disasters and to the planning for such incidents as emergency planning.

Defining Disasters

Before emergency planning can commence it is necessary to define the events which will bring the emergency plans into effect. A number of organisations have attempted to define such events as follows:

> ... an abnormal situation which, to limit damage to persons, property or the environment, requires prompt action beyond normal procedures.[1]

> ... an event which afflicts a community, the consequences of which are beyond the immediate financial, material or emotional resources of the community.[2]

> ... any emergency situation in which normal life is thrown suddenly into confusion; the population, as a result, having need of protection, food, clothing,

shelter, medical attention, social care and other essentials.[3]

The problem with these definitions is that they are highly subjective and depend on a judgement of the incident and of the resources available to meet it. Not surprisingly, therefore, it is often very difficult for persons responding to an incident to classify it, particularly at an early stage. Similar problems are created for planners who are attempting to plan for events which are of unknown origin, with an unknown frequency and identifiable only by a subjective definition of their effects.

In order to establish a basis for planning, emergency planners have traditionally divided disasters into three main types – natural, technological and planned. *Natural disasters* are normally violent natural events which have an extreme impact on human beings. Typical examples are floods, storms, earthquakes and volcanoes. *Technological disasters* usually involve the failure of technological systems and are often blamed on human error. Typical examples include transportation accidents, fires, explosions and the release of hazardous materials. *Planned disasters* are caused by deliberate destructive human actions and typical examples are terrorist bombings and civil disturbances such as rioting.

To these traditional disaster types a fourth type has been added in recent years, namely *ecological disasters*. Unlike other disasters these are usually slow and insidious but ultimately they may be the most destructive. Typical examples include the Oklahoma Dust Bowl of the 1920s, the 'greenhouse effect', and the massive air pollution caused by the burning of oil wells after the Gulf War.

This traditional approach to categorising disasters has in recent years been questioned as inadequate, particularly in developed countries where most disasters appear to involve a multiplicity of causes. A 1990 publication of the London Emergency Planning Information Centre argues that the central issue in a disaster is not the causal agent but rather the vulnerability of the situation in which it occurs.[4] The cause of a disaster may vary from an earthquake to a cigarette dropped in a London tube station but whether a disaster occurs and the extent of any disaster which does occur is a function of the vulnerability of the people involved. The effect of a disaster in this scenario is therefore a function of the interrelationship between the cause, the vulnerability inherent in the situation, and the resources available to cope with the effects of the disaster. It is the view of the author that this argument has considerable merit and should be taken on board by emergency planners, particularly in the developed countries, where 'simple' disasters are more and more unlikely to occur.

The concept of vulnerability is neatly illustrated by an examination of the two major earthquakes, each measuring 6.9 on the Richter Scale, which occurred in Armenia in December 1988 and San Francisco in October 1989. The Armenian earthquake resulted in approximately 800 deaths and 300,000 injuries and the survivors waited for days in the open for relief to arrive from the West. The San Francisco earthquake on the other hand caused approximately 61 deaths and 400 injuries and damage to buildings was limited.

The different results of these two similar earthquakes was a function of the different inherent vulnerabilities in each area before the disasters occurred and the different resources available to deal with the disasters when they struck. In California engineering design of earthquake resistant buildings has been practised for many years and is now at an advanced stage. In Armenia, on the other hand, much of the population lived in apartment blocks which 'not only lacked steel reinforcement but also had poorly designed joints and low quality concrete'.[5] The resources available locally in Armenia could not of course compare with the resources of California, one of the wealthiest regions of the world.

Conceptualising Disasters

As well as the difficulty of categorising disasters, emergency planners also have difficulty in conceptualising events which are totally diverse, extremely rare and not available anywhere for inspection or examination. A common response to this limitation is to conceptualise disasters in terms which are familiar to the planner, that is, as larger versions of standard accidents. This approach is not surprising since, as has already been mentioned, much emergency planning flows from the 'normal' emergency services. However, Tierney and Quarantelli argue strongly that this approach, although common, is inherently flawed and that disasters are different from large accidents not only in degree but also in kind.[6] Emergency planners, therefore, should be encouraged to 'break out' of their existing mind-set in which they prepare for disasters that will occur at arm's length and during which the emergency services will be stretched but retain control. They must instead try to plan for incidents where the emergency services may themselves be within the disaster area, where the emergency services will often be overwhelmed and where standard operating procedures will be totally inadequate.

This process can be facilitated by the use of a simple tool which was developed by Western in the early 1970s.[7] This tool, which is illustrated in Figure 1, depicts the five distinct

Figure 1: Spatial zones of a disaster

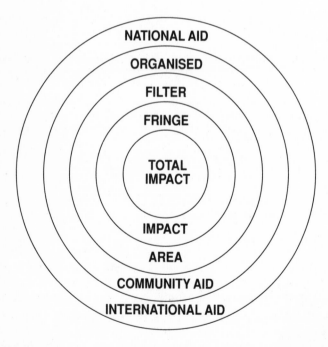

Source: Western, K.A., 'The Epidemiology of Natural and Manmade Disasters – The Present State of the Art', University of London Dissertation (1972).

spatial zones of a disaster as a series of concentric rings. The circular configuration of the zones is of course not to be taken literally but their concentric relationship to one another is useful in conceptualising the disaster scene. The five spatial zones are described as:

1. The zone of total impact, which receives the full force of the disaster and where destruction and death are most severe.
2. The zone of fringe impact, which is directly affected by the disaster but where damage and casualties are considerably less.
3. The zone of filtration, which escapes the disaster and into which the injured and homeless will tend to filter.
4. The zone of organised community aid, from which organised emergency personnel and services will arrive to assist in the disaster.
5. The zone of national and international aid, which will vary in size depending on the extent of the disaster and from which organised assistance will be provided if required.

Unfortunately, most emergency planning is based on the scenario of a small zone of total impact to which assistance can be provided from the local emergency services which are usually considered to be located in the zone of organised community aid. Plans based on this scenario could be entirely upset if the zone of total impact included large sections of the emergency services and it is vital that this possibility is considered in all emergency planning.

Frequency of Disasters

A pressing question of interest to governments and emergency planners is whether or not the frequency of disasters is on the increase. The subjective definitions of disaster make this issue a particularly difficult one to resolve statistically, although the alarming trend of serious incidents in the United Kingdom during the 1980s (see Appendix 2) left few people there in doubt on the matter. There are also certain objective indications, including much publicised losses at Lloyd's of London, which support the suggestion that disasters are on the increase.

Keller, Wilson and Kara-Zaitri of the University of Bradford have attempted to address this question by the development of the so-called Bradford Disaster Scale.[8] This scale, which is similar to the Richter Scale for earthquakes, categorises the magnitude of disasters by the logarithm to the base 10 of the number of fatalities. Thus a disaster with 10 fatalities is magnitude 1, 100 fatalities magnitude 2, and so on. Using this scale the Bradford researchers examined the frequency of disasters in Europe at ten-year intervals for the period 1888-1988. The graph of this data, as shown in Figure 2, reveals a gradual increase for the first eighty years, followed by a much more rapid increase over the final twenty-year period. The corresponding graph of data for disasters in the United Kingdom (Figure 3) indicates a more erratic pattern but with a quite noticeable increase over the last ten-year period.

Figure 2: European disasters: ten-year period analysis

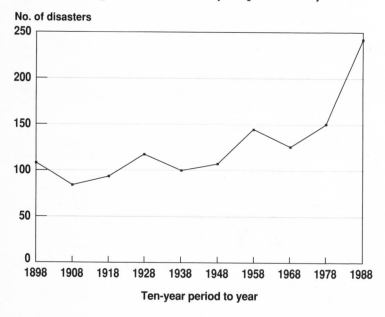

Source: Keller, A.Z., Wilson, H. and Kara-Zaitri, C., 'The Bradford Disaster Scale', *Disaster Management,* Volume 2, No. 4, 1990.

The Bradford Scale has been criticised by Horlick-Jones and Peters on a number of issues.[9] The use of the number of dead as the only measure of disasters results in the

Figure 3: United Kingdom disasters: ten-year period analysis

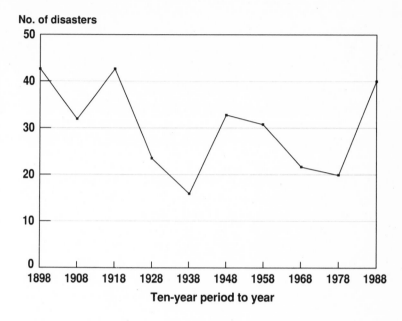

Source: Keller, A.Z., Wilson, H. and Kara-Zaitri, C., 'The Bradford Disaster Scale', *Disaster Management*, Volume 2, No. 4, 1990.

omission of many real disasters from the scale. To illustrate this argument they quote two modern disasters which are excluded from analysis by the Bradford method. These are the Cannon Street train crash, which resulted in two deaths and two hundred and forty-eight injuries and which seriously stretched the London emergency services, and the 1976 Seveso Dioxin accident in northern Italy, where there were no fatalities but hundreds of injured and where a long-term evacuation of the area was required.

Another issue is the use of the log scale which tends to devalue human life by, for instance, rating thirty-two deaths as a disaster of magnitude 1.5 and one thousand deaths as a disaster of magnitude 3.0. Overall it can be argued that the Bradford Scale attempts to capture in simple numeric form a highly complex socio-economic phenomenon and as such is essentially inadequate. The fact that the Bradford Scale has been largely ignored by disaster researchers and writers outside of Bradford would seem to indicate general agreement with this criticism.

Future Vulnerabilities

For a country such as Ireland, which has not been subjected to regular natural disasters, the frequency of future disasters will depend largely on the extent to which the population becomes more or less vulnerable. The trend towards increasing use of technology will help to reduce the risk that human error might lead to disaster in many situations. For example, the fitting of radios on all train engines should help to prevent the recurrence of an incident similar to that which occurred at Cherryville on the outskirts of Kildare in 1983 when a train, which ran out of fuel, was unable to contact the train following behind.

However increased use of technology can bring its own vulnerabilities as society becomes more and more dependant on technology. This concept has been described as 'the Titanic Syndrome' on the basis that that ship might still be afloat if the captain had not believed that it was unsinkable.[10] Of particular concern is the projected absence of humans from many critical decision-making processes in the future, which will remove a significant degree of flexibility and will tend to make the environment much less 'forgiving' of error. Complete faith in technology can be misplaced; the London Emergency Planning Information Centre study, for instance, cites a major failure in the computer that controls all air traffic over Heathrow Airport which was subsequently attributed to a twenty-year-old software 'bug'.[11]

A further cause for concern for the future is the growing number and dispersal of toxic substances. In 1980 Foster stated that approximately 50 million tons of more than 1,700 hazardous materials were transported in Britain every year, resulting in over 200 annual incidents causing road closures and traffic delays.[12] The corresponding figures for Ireland would, of course, be substantially lower but the Merck Sharpe and Dohme versus Hanrahan controversy shows there is no room for complacency. In 1988 Mitroff stated that since 1900 there had been twenty-nine major industrial accidents worldwide involving more that fifty deaths, and that half of those incidents had occurred within the previous eight years.[13] The sobering thought from an Irish point of view is that one of those incidents occurred in Bantry Bay when the Betelgeuse oil tanker exploded at the Whiddy Oil Terminal in 1979.

Justification of Expenditure on Emergency Planning

Given the many difficulties involved, the wisdom of invest-
ing time and resources in emergency planning may be
subject to question in some quarters. However, there are a
number of reasons why an appropriate level of emergency
planning is both necessary and worthwhile. Firstly, there is a
moral obligation to the potential victims of future disasters.
Emergency planning will not prevent all disasters and in the
case of disasters which do occur it may not prevent all loss of
life. However, proper emergency planning will improve the
response of the emergency services and since that
improvement is likely to result in the saving of life and/or
the reduction of suffering during a disaster, then the
process is surely justified.

Secondly, it is possible to predict with certainty that any
future disaster will be followed by a public search for scapegoats who can be blamed for any perceived inadequacies in
the emergency response. This search for scapegoats may be
carried on through the media, liability actions by victims, by
a tribunal of enquiry, or most likely by all three. The
aftermath of the Stardust and Whiddy disasters gave ample
evidence of the thoroughness with which every aspect of a
disaster is likely to be dissected and examined. In that
situation an organisation which has developed emergency
planning to the maximum extent possible within its
resources will not only have the advantage of a good
response to the disaster but can also point to its planning
efforts as a defence against any accusations of carelessness.

Finally an argument for emergency planning can be made
on a cost–benefit basis. Once a disaster occurs, the need for
spending is undeniable but the costs at that stage are generally
high. These costs include the payroll costs involved in the
deployment of large numbers of emergency personnel as well
as expenditure on materials and the hire of specialist
equipment during the crisis phase. Following the immediate
crisis there are the medical costs of caring for the injured,
which may continue for years, and the cost of any necessary
repairs and replacement of infrastructure, buildings and
equipment. Finally there is the loss of productive output, both
in the short term as a result of the disaster effect and in the
long term with the loss of productive community members.
Emergency planning, on the other hand, is a management

rather than a resource-based process and the costs involved therefore are relatively small. Furthermore, even in the absence of disasters, many aspects of emergency planning are beneficial to the organisations involved. The complex cost and probability calculations required to show that investment in emergency planning is cost effective are outside the scope of this study but intuitively it would appear that it must be so.

−2−

Literature Review

Research for this study indicated a paucity of readily available material relevant to emergency planning, although there are indications that this situation may be in the process of changing. (Much of the available material, moreover, is not directly related to emergency planning in Ireland but is most often concerned with the regulations pertaining to the process in different countries. The material which is relevant has been reviewed under the following headings: responses to recent disasters; crisis planning/management; and disaster research.

Responses to Recent Disasters

Reports on the *response* to disasters, as opposed to reports *on* disasters, have traditionally been constrained by a number of issues. There is a natural wish not to cause further distress to survivors or to relatives of victims. There can also be a reluctance to examine the disaster response too closely on the grounds that any such examination might reveal unpalatable details and could end as a process of apportioning blame, which might have very damaging consequences for everyone involved. Nevertheless, these reports do provide a useful starting point for any study of emergency planning.

British Reports

The series of disasters that occurred during the 1980s in the United Kingdom has generated a significant number of journal articles and conference papers, many of which were written by emergency service professionals who were involved in the disaster responses. This literature details the fire brigade, police, ambulance and hospital response to a series of incidents including the Kegworth air crash, the

Zeebrugge ferry disaster and many more. Not surprisingly, many of the contributions tend to be specialised and descriptive of what happened (or perhaps what the participants like to believe happened). There is usually no critical analysis of the overall performance of the service involved or, more significantly, of the level of co-ordination between the services. In many ways it is similar to history as written by the winners. This author has seen no contribution describing the success or otherwise of the emergency plans used during any of these disasters.

Notwithstanding the above limitations, these reports are of interest to this study for a number of reasons. The events which they describe in a neighbouring country illustrate the potential vulnerability of Ireland to the occurrence of similar disasters and as such they underline the need for emergency planning. Furthermore they have brought to light a number of issues which might otherwise not have achieved prominence.

One of these concerns the long-term psychological effects of disasters on survivors and emergency service workers. Numerous reports mention nightmares, depression and sleeplessness among survivors and the emergency service personnel who have been exposed to horrific experiences in the aftermath of disasters.[1] Summarising much of the work in this area Duckworth points out that many of the emergency services have a 'macho' culture which can make it difficult for an individual to admit to a problem and seek help.[2] He recommends that all emergency service personnel who are likely to ever become involved in a disaster situation should receive special training. This training should establish that post traumatic stress disorder (PTSD) is a 'normal' experience and should introduce the type of screening and counselling that would be used after a disaster to assist those who might need help.

Another feature of recent British disasters, which is conspicuous by its absence from much of the literature, is the growing phenomenon of criminal and civil prosecution of persons or organisations which are held to be responsible for the death and injury of disaster victims. In the cases of the Zeebrugge ferry disaster and the Clapham Junction train crash commercial pressures appear to have caused a reduction in safety standards and, as a result, criminal proceedings were initiated against the ferry company and British Rail respectively.

However, in the case of the Hillsborough Football Ground disaster a police decision appears to have been a critical factor in the tragedy and therefore it was one of the emergency services which was placed in the dock, particularly by the media. This has raised the spectre of future disasters resulting in legal liability suits against the emergency services for actions which they may have taken, or failed to take, during the course of a disaster response. In a slightly exaggerated comment on this phenomenon the *Sunday Times* stated that 'since the abolition of capital punishment the British public has turned to those in charge during lurid disasters to sate its lust for retribution'.[3]

The Heysel Stadium Disaster

In contrast to many of the reports on British disasters a conference paper by Hart and Pijnenburg on the Heysel Stadium disaster gives an incisive view of many of the problems faced by the emergency services on that occasion.[4] On 28 May 1985 Liverpool and Juventus were due to play in the European Champions Cup Final at the Heysel Stadium, Brussels. A series of events conspired to create a vulnerability which was subsequently exposed with tragic consequences. Carelessness in the sale of tickets for a supposedly neutral area of the stadium brought Italian and English fans together in adjoining sections. Inadequate fencing between the sections and a low level of policing completed the pre-disaster scenario. Fifty minutes before the game was due to begin a group of Liverpool fans launched a massive attack on the Italians in the adjoining section. In the resulting stampede thirty-eight people were killed and more than 400 injured.

As the disaster unfolded a number of key decisions were made, sometimes by default, by a small group of officials who were present in the stadium. Faced with rampaging Liverpool supporters, large numbers of dead and injured, and rioting Juventus fans at the opposite end of the stadium, decisions concerning emergency relief, law and order and football all became intermingled. The decisions to allow the football match to proceed and not to attempt mass arrests of troublemakers, which were both taken with a view to preventing even more serious disturbances, were subsequently heavily criticised within Belgium and internationally. However, from the perspective of those who made the decisions they were, in fact, basically sound since they facilitated the recovery and treatment of the injured and their subsequent removal to hospital.

Hart and Pijnenburg have listed a series of factors which militated against an optimum response by the emergency services to the Heysel disaster. Firstly, the Belgian Gendarmerie are organised along hierarchical lines where vertical communication is strictly on a level by level basis. The absence of an officer from one of these levels as the incident began created confusion and prevented a redeployment of personnel at a time when the situation might have been brought under control. Secondly, there were a number of technical problems with communication equipment which contributed to the confusion. Finally, an ongoing conflict between the Gendarmerie and other emergency agencies in the Brussels area surfaced during the disaster in the form of disputes over priorities. At one stage, for example, a major row developed over priority access to the stadium between the commander of the Gendarmerie, intent on restoring order, and the commander of the fire brigade who wished to rescue some of the trapped victims. This is the only disaster report in which the author has seen interservice rivalry discussed, although the topic has surfaced regularly during informal discussions on emergency planning. For that reason alone this paper is of particular interest in the context of emergency planning in Ireland.

Irish Reports

In Ireland the major disasters of recent years included the Stardust fire, the Whiddy Oil Terminal explosion and the Air India crash (see Appendix 1). The Stardust and Whiddy disasters resulted in formal Tribunals of Inquiry which investigated the incidents without regard to time or cost. The Whiddy Tribunal report is concerned largely with the safety of oil tankers in Irish waters and many of its recommendations could be regarded as disaster mitigation.[5] However it makes no recommendations on the organisation of the emergency services.

The Stardust Tribunal report does refer to the Eastern Health Board's Major Accident Plan, as the emergency plan was known at that time.[6] The report does not comment on the effectiveness or otherwise of the plan and makes no recommendation on future emergency plans or emergency planning in general. This is in sharp contrast to extensive recommendations in the areas of building regulations and the organisation of the fire service.

The only report, of which this author is aware, on the implementation of an emergency plan in Ireland is a Southern Health Board report on the implementation of its Major Accident Plan during the Air India disaster.[7] This incident was not typical of disasters in the British Isles in that there were no survivors and the incident was entirely external to the local area, that is, there was no damage to the local infrastructure and there were no local victims. The report indicates that the Major Accident Plan was activated and operated smoothly: 131 bodies were recovered and removed to the Cork Regional Hospital; pathological and radiological services were provided for each body; co-operation was provided to the Gardaí in their forensic work; relatives of the victims were received and facilitated in the identification of the bodies; visits by Irish, Canadian and Indian government representatives were arranged; and the press was kept fully briefed throughout.

This incident was not, of course, a full test of the plan but in as far as the plan was tested, it appears to have operated successfully. Interestingly, although the health board's Major Accident Plan did not mention any special management arrangements, a five person incident management group was established at the Regional Hospital. This group, which included the chief executive officer of the health board, continually assessed the situation throughout the period of the crisis, made all necessary decisions, liaised with key internal and external groups and set tasks and objectives for each phase of the response. The experience of this group is a strong argument in favour of pre-selected crisis management teams.

Crisis Planning/Management

Since Fayol listed planning as one of the five key functions of management[8] much has been written in the management literature on different types of planning, including short and long-term planning, operational and contingency planning, and personal and corporate planning. All planning involves forecasts and assumptions about the future and therefore most planning models include some type of circular or iterative process whereby assumptions are checked and plans modified as required. A typical model, proposed by Richardson and Richardson, is circular in shape and involves a continuous process including the following stages: define issue, collect relevant data, develop alternative solutions, assess consequences, select optimum solution, implement solution, measure results, define issue . . .[9] Many writers have attempted to define planning, and the definition regarded as most relevant to this study is that proposed by Warren:

> Planning is essentially a process of preparing for the commitment of resources in the most economical fashion and, by preparing, of allowing this commitment to be made faster and less disruptively.[10]

A series of events during the past fifteen years which seriously threatened the existence of a number of large commercial organisations has focused attention on a variant of contingency planning that has become known as crisis planning or more usually as crisis management. These incidents included the fatal leak of poison gas from the Union Carbide plant in Bhopal, the introduction of cyanide capsules into packages of Tylenol, and the contamination of its product with benzene which threatened to destroy the Perrier brand name. In general writers on this topic tend to concentrate their attention on four main areas: the predictability of many crises, the need for crisis planning, decision making during crises and dealing with the media.

Predictability of Many Crises

Mitroff[11] and Fink[12] both argue that most major disasters can be identified in advance by companies which systematically search for the correct signals. Fink examines a series of incidents including the destruction of the ill-fated Challenger space shuttle and, using internal memos, shows that NASA had ample warning of the disaster. It can be argued that this approach is easy with the benefit of hindsight but there is an underlying truth involved which is worthy of attention. In the case of private corporations Weick and others advise the development of corporate cultures which emphasise safety and reliability.[13] These cultures should promote bottom-up communication processes which would allow warning signals to reach those in positions of influence. This concept also has relevance for public emergency organisations in Ireland. For example, how many local authority or health board chief executives can be confident that minor chemical spills or a series of food poisoning cases would be correctly interpreted within their organisations as signals of potentially greater events ?

Mitroff proposes that the complex scenarios created by the large number and variety of potential threats facing many organisations can be rationalised by the use of a 'crisis portfolio'. This involves the grouping together of all possible crises according to their underlying structural similarity; thus families of crises are created which include all potential crises of a particular type. In the case of a manufacturing organisation this concept is illustrated by a group consisting of breakdowns in products, plants, packages and equipment. Mitroff recommends that at least one crisis from each family is chosen and that planning for that crisis is carried out within the organisation.

Such an approach has merit in the context of Irish emergency planning where many potential disasters can be grouped relatively easily. For example, disasters involving passenger aircraft, trains and buses form a natural group; likewise air pollution, contamination of water supplies and the adultera-tion of food form another group. It seems obvious that any organisation which has prepared effectively for an aircraft crash will, most likely, perform well in the event of a train accident.

Need for Crisis Planning

Crises in commercial organisations are similar in many ways to disasters: the information available for decision making is usually inadequate, there is never enough time to consult with all interested parties, potential solutions often have a significant downside and bad decisions can threaten the viability of the organisation. Mitroff and Fink both contend that an organisation can facilitate the successful resolution of crises by making the following preparations:

1. assemble a crisis management team
2. provide training for members of the team
3. prepare crisis management plans.

Members of crisis management teams should be carefully chosen to provide a good balance and each member should have a designated alternate. The crisis management plans cannot of course include detailed instructions on how each crisis is to be handled but they can address certain predictable issues such as the nomination of the organisation's spokesperson and decisions on the management of the non-crisis aspects of the business during the crisis. The logic of this approach is that effective crisis management plans should predetermine all possible lower order decisions, releasing managers, who have been specially trained, to deal with the more unpredictable and difficult aspects of the crisis. At the same time other managers would tend to the routine business of the company.

Fink argues that in the event of a crisis occurring, the benefits to companies that have effective crisis management strategies in place are exceptional. To support this claim he quotes a survey of Fortune 500 companies which showed that for organisations without a crisis management plan the aftereffects of a crisis lasted about two and a half times longer than for those that did have a plan. Similar benefits could be expected to accrue to Irish emergency service organisations.

Decision Making During Crises

Crises are stressful occasions and therefore usually involve decision making under stress. Fink examines the relationship between stress and decision making and for optimum decisions recommends a state of mind which he describes as 'vigilant'. This state of mind allows the decision maker to painstakingly search for all relevant information, assimilate that information and carefully weigh alternative choices before making a decision. The vigilant type of decision maker is illustrated by reference to the four alternatives which result in poor quality decisions as follows:

1. Unconflicted inertia: this decision maker ignores information on associated risks and continues with the status quo. This situation may involve the 'it can't happen here' syndrome.
2. Unconflicted change: this decision maker follows the last advice which he or she has heard and tends to take the path of least resistance.

3. Defensive avoidance: this decision maker avoids decision making by continually proposing and examining a myriad of possible alternatives, 'paralysis by analysis'.
4. Hyper vigilance: this decision maker is in a state of panic and is the one most likely to make major mistakes. The full range of alternatives and their associated consequences are often overlooked as extreme stress causes a condition known as cognitive constriction or 'blinkered vision'.

Fink argues that there are a number of steps that organisations can take to ensure that their managers will achieve the desired vigilant state during times of crisis. The existence of a crisis management plan which resolves many of the low-level problems of the crisis will ease the pressure on the decision makers. Critical decisions should not be made in isolation by a manager but rather in conjunction with a team, which acts as a check on the decisions. The crisis management team should engage in brainstorming and thus bring to the surface all possible solutions so that they can be examined and the optimum solution chosen. Simple illustrative devices such as decision tree diagrams can be of particular assistance. Crisis management teams should be 'inoculated' against stress by means of crisis simulation workshops and exercises. Managers must be taught to avoid causing unnecessary stress in crisis situations by futile questioning of the reasons why the crisis has occurred. Instead the crisis should be accepted for what it is and all energies devoted to resolving it.

Dealing with the Media

When crisis strikes a commercial organisation the most valuable asset which is threatened is usually the organisation's reputation. That reputation can be destroyed or enhanced by a public perception of the manner in which the crisis arose and was subsequently dealt with. In the late twentieth century public perceptions are usually formed by the media and therefore it is understandable that commercial organisations in crisis situations should be highly sensitive to the media treatment of their difficulties. Not surprisingly the literature on crisis management pays particular attention to this topic and Nelkin[14] and Scanlon[15] suggest a number of key issues which are vital in this area.

For larger crises in particular the media is a twenty-four hour multinational industry with an insatiable appetite for information. Most members of the media, however, operate to tight deadlines and therefore organisations can retain some control by quickly making available a spokesperson who is readily accessible and who can provide reporters with the information they require in a usable form. This spokesperson must be seen to have access to the key figures within the organisation and in that situation the organisation has a good chance of having its point of view reflected in the media coverage. For example, where bad news is inevitable the organisation can put it in a context which will tend to lessen the damage to the organisation's reputation. Stonewalling, either by making no spokesperson available or by putting forward a spokesperson who has no useful information, will not suppress a story. On the contrary it will tend to promote rumours which can only damage the organisation and when the story is eventually exposed it may appear in a context that is highly unfavourable.

When minute quantities of benzene were discovered in Perrier products in North Carolina the company was faced with an information dilemma. The problem could have been caused by product tampering in the United States or by contamination at the bottling plant in France. Unfortunately the tests required to identify the source of the problem took forty-eight hours and in the interim period the company attempted to stonewall the media. During this period a company spokesperson, facing a barrage of questions, made an off-the-cuff remark that the problem could have been caused by a 'greasy rag'. In the absence of any other information the 'greasy rag' story was run by the international media causing serious damage to the Perrier reputation for purity.

All authorities appear to agree that crisis management plans should include a section on communications and that the organisation's spokesperson should be a member of the crisis management team. The spokesperson should have received training in communications so that the organisation's view is put across with the optimum effect, particularly on television where the appearance, demeanour and style of the spokesperson can often be as important as what is said.

At all costs organisations must avoid dishonesty in their dealings with the media. Fink is quite definite on this issue when he states that 'being dishonest or less than honest with the media will only escalate your crisis into proportions that will stagger you. It will serve to destroy your present and future credibility with the media.'[16] To illustrate this argument Fink quotes a number of cases including the Three Mile Island nuclear plant crisis when the plant operators, Metropolitan Edison, attempted to play down the crisis by issuing radiation figures which were substantially lower than those which had been measured. Within hours the deception was discovered by the media with devastating consequences for the company's reputation which later made it very difficult for the company to persuade the public and the regulatory agencies that the reactor was in fact under control and that the crisis was at an end.

For emergency organisations in Ireland it is clear that an authoritative spokesperson who has received some training in communications, who is available to the media throughout the crisis and who is seen to have access to up-to-date information can be of great help in preventing damaging rumours and in controlling the flow of necessary information to the public.

Disaster Research

In recent years academic research into disasters has been initiated at a number of universities around the world. However the major centres of research are still in the United States at the Disaster Research Centre at the University of Delaware and the Natural Hazards Research and Applications Information Centre at the University of Colorado. For many years disaster research in the United States was dominated by sociologists who studied the behaviour of people and organisations during disasters and geographers who studied the patterns of human settlement which tended to place communities at risk. Today disaster research is a multidisciplinary field, and with the addition of specialists from the fields of organisational behaviour and public administration, results are becoming available which are of interest to emergency planners.

Features of Modern Disasters

Comfort,[17] Rosenthal,[18] Quarantelli[19] and others have described certain common features of modern disasters which can be summarised as follows:

1. The environment of a disaster is usually highly complex as one set of events triggers another in a reciprocal interactive sequence. A failure to appreciate this interactive nature of events can often result in the emergency services themselves becoming involved in disasters as happened during the Sandoz fire in Basle and at Hillsborough.
2. Disasters cannot normally be handled effectively by any one organisation and thus the typical disaster response is characterised as interorganisational. This can lead to complications with organisations which perceive themselves to be in competition during normal times, usually for resources.
3. Disasters generate a massive inflow of people beginning usually with the arrival of large numbers of volunteers followed by the media, anxious relatives, disaster tourists and dignitaries (who are usually more of a hindrance than a help).
4. Disaster situations usually involve an overloading of the means of communication and this is partially responsible for the usual failure of decision makers to obtain an overall view of what is occurring.
5. Disaster environments generally require decisions of the highest quality since human life is often at stake. However two of the ingredients usually regarded as necessary for optimum decision making, adequate information and sufficient time, are normally not available.
6. Disasters usually involve an altering of performance criteria for the emergency services. Choices are often required between deserving alternatives and, with limited resources, work must be prioritised in those areas where it will be most effective. In the case of medical practitioners this may involve ignoring victims close to death so that those with a chance of living can be helped.
7. Most disasters are major events in the societies in which they occur and as such can have significant consequences for the local social and political fabric. It is not uncommon for disasters to destroy the careers of politicians and/or public servants.

Organisational Effectiveness

Mileti and Sorensen of the University of Colorado have summarised the findings of research at that institution on the effectiveness of organisations during low probability catastrophic events.[20] They list the chief factors which indicate an effective response by an individual organisation as:

1. The extent to which the organisation's functions in a disaster correspond to its normal functions.
2. The extent to which the organisation can be flexible in its operating procedures and structures.
3. The ability of the organisation to decide what needs to be done and how to prioritise the work.
4. Access to adequate resources.
5. The ability to collect and share information.
6. Approval and recognition by other organisations of the organisation's role in emergency-related work.

They also list the factors which indicate an effective response by groups of organisations as:

1. The degree to which each organisation knows what it and other organisations are to do during the emergency.
2. The extent to which organisations responding to an emergency are co-ordinated.
3. The quality of the communication process.
4. The extent to which individual organisations are prepared to give up some degree of autonomy in order to facilitate a co-ordinated response.

Success Factors

E.L. Quarantelli of the University of Delaware, one of the foremost authorities on disasters in the English-speaking world, argues that research at that institution would indicate that the success of any organisation in a disaster will hinge on its ability to deal with certain predictable problems which arise in the areas of: the communication process; the exercise of authority and decision making; and the development of co-ordination.[21]

Communication Process

In the area of communication major problems arise with *what* is communicated rather than *how* it is communicated. The preoccupation of emergency planners with the physical means of communication, therefore, is usually at the expense of consideration of the organisational problems connected with information flow. Problems with communication arise in five different areas as follows:

1. Internal organisational information flow is disrupted by an overloading of the existing system and a breaking of the usual vertical chain of command along which information normally flows up and down.
2. Information flow between organisations is a problem as contact is established with individuals with whom there has been no pre-disaster relationship.
3. Information flow from organisations to the general public is usually poor because of a failure to understand the information requirements of the public.
4. Information flow from the public to organisations usually results in an overload of the switchboards in high visibility organisations and a resulting failure to obtain critical information.
5. Information flow within systems of organisations should be a multiple two-way process but unfortunately many organisations see the process as one way only.

Exercise of Authority and Decision Making

Research would indicate that lines of authority do not break down in established organisations during disasters. Where higher officials cannot be contacted the tendency has been for people on the spot to make the required decisions even where such decisions would normally be outside their range of competence. The fear that key personnel might desert their responsibilities to take care of their own families has not been borne out in practice and there are usually few problems concerning the authority of different organisations to deal with those tasks which are their traditional responsibility. Problems with decision making arise in the following areas:

1. The tendency of key officials in positions of authority to continue working too long, leading to their collapse and a possible breakdown in authority.
2. Difficulties in determining who has the authority to perform new disaster-related tasks.

3. Organisational domain conflicts, for example between established organisations and emerging community groups.
4. Jurisdictional differences which occur when disasters cut across the boundaries of organisations.

Development of Co-ordination

The usual assumption of planners and managers that centralised control has to be imposed from the top down on emergency activities is incorrect: it is co-ordination, not control, that is required. However, while most organisations subscribe to the principle of co-ordination, the following problems usually conspire against its achievement:

1. A lack of consensus between organisations as to the meaning of co-ordination, with some organisations viewing co-ordination as merely informing others of what they are doing.
2. Strained organisational relationships which develop over the execution of new disaster tasks even among local agencies which are accustomed to working together.
3. The large number of organisations responding to major disasters.

Implications

The above research results are significant for Irish emergency planners in that they indicate the part which written plans can play in an effective disaster response. In particular co-ordinated plans can help to clarify the roles of the different organisations and achieve interorganisational recognition for these roles. However, the research results make it clear that this is but a portion of the overall planning process. The full process involves detailed task specification and the creation of links between different groups both within individual organisations and within groups of organisations. In practical terms this process can only be advanced within organisations by means of training and particularly by the organisation of exercises.

The interorganisational part of the process requires extensive meetings, two-way communication and ongoing contacts. This communication process can be given substance by sharing certain disaster-related resources and by jointly organising exercises. The end result of the process should be the creation of a climate and an attitude which are favourable to coping with disasters. This is of course a much wider process than the writing of plans. As Quarantelli emphasises: 'the existence of a written document can actually be dysfunctional or dangerous. It may mislead officials into thinking that they are prepared for disaster because an official plan exists.'[22]

—3—

International Perspective

Commitment to Emergency Planning

Emergency planning is practised in many countries around the world under different names and with various levels of commitment. In most countries emergency planning is promoted and supported by governments and thus there is a natural tendency for governments to accentuate the progress that has been achieved. Since the results of emergency planning are not easy to measure, it can be difficult for an outside observer to distinguish, in all cases, between real disaster preparedness and nominal or 'paper' planning. In as much as it can be ascertained, the level of commitment to emergency planning in individual countries appears to be mainly related to the intensity of the perceived threat of disasters and the resources available for emergency planning. Not surprisingly, therefore, it is among the wealthy countries of the world, and particularly those threatened by disasters, that emergency planning appears to be most developed.

Threats of Disaster

Major destruction and loss of life in natural disasters is nowadays associated in particular with Third World countries. Here, any emergency planning which does take place tends to be largely concerned with attempts at forecasting disasters and the provision of disaster warnings to the public. However, several of the world's developed countries are also subject to a wide spectrum of natural disasters (see Appendix 3). For example Japan and the west coast of the United States are both included in the Pacific 'Ring of Fire' and therefore subject to severe seismic activity.

In the United States this activity includes earthquakes, such as occurred in California in 1989, volcanoes, such as the 1980 Mount St Helen's eruption, and tsunamis which are massive waves caused by undersea earthquakes. All of these are overshadowed by the threat of a catastrophic earthquake which has been predicted for California for many years now. The United States is also subject to regular flooding disasters, tornadoes and hurricanes. The scale of these disasters is indicated by the fact that in five of the ten years between 1970 and 1980 the US Congress spent more than one billion dollars on disaster relief.[1] Within the European Community there are threats of flooding, earthquakes, forest fires and avalanches, particularly in the countries of southern Europe.

In all developed countries there are threats of technological disaster, particularly in the areas of passenger transport accidents, accidents within the chemical and nuclear industries and accidents during the transport of hazardous substances. In recent years these have been augmented by the post-Chernobyl threat of transnational disasters. The threat of chemical accidents is of particular concern in countries such as Holland where one million people live in the Greater Rotterdam area surrounding Europe's largest concentration of oil refineries, chemical plants and associated transport infrastructure.

The potential for disaster in Britain appears to have been exacerbated during the past ten years by economic decline and a resulting lack of necessary investment. For example, lack of private investment in the two stadia can be linked directly to the Bradford and Hillsborough disasters. A corresponding lack of investment in the public sector, particularly public transport, can be seen as a major long-term cause of recent transport disasters such as the King's Cross escalator fire and the Clapham Junction train crash. To these 'conventional' technological threats can be added the unforeseeable disasters such as threatened Canada in 1978 when the space satellite COSMOS 954 scattered radioactive debris over the North West Territories.

Emergency Planning and Civil Defence

Emergency planning has been promoted in many countries by the threat, or perceived threat, of war. Thus in countries such as Israel, where a 'seige mentality' is a part of the national culture, emergency planning tends to be highly developed. This level of preparedness was graphically demonstrated during the Gulf War when gas masks were distributed to the entire population of Israel in a speedy and efficient operation. Specific emergency planning for wartime conditions is more usually referred to as civil defence and is not included in this study. However in recent years the lines between civil defence and emergency planning have become blurred in many countries, notably the United Kingdom.

In the post-war era the British government was acutely conscious of the vulnerability of its citizens to a Soviet nuclear strike and therefore civil defence was promoted extensively. All local authorities were empowered to employ civil defence officers and all spending on civil defence could be recouped from central government. This resulted in an extensive network of civil defence officers employed at local level with a Civil Defence College to provide training. The easing of East–West tensions and a reluctance on the part of many Labour controlled local authorities to engage in civil defence has made this infrastructure increasingly irrelevant in recent years. As a result there has been a gradual move, at least in nominal terms, from civil defence to emergency planning. Civil defence officers are now known as emergency planning officers and the Civil Defence College is known as the Emergency Planning College. However the main Home Office guidance document on emergency planning for local authorities is still largely concerned with traditional civil defence issues.[2] The collapse of communism is Eastern Europe and the concurrent demise of the Warsaw Pact should result in a further transfer of emphasis from civil defence to emergency planning in Britain. Otherwise the annual cost of the Civil Emergency Service at £128 million, or £2.26 per head of population, cannot logically be justified.[3]

All Hazards Approach

In many areas of the world emergency planning began as a form of preparation for specific threats, such as flooding. However in most countries today the basis of emergency planning is the 'all hazards' approach, which as the name implies involves a single planning process for almost all possible threats. This approach has facilitated the merger of emergency planning and civil defence in countries such as Britain since the nuclear threat can be regarded as one of the hazards. It has the advantage of greatly simplifying the planning process and also facilitates cross-community support. In real terms it is a recognition that the physical and organisational resources available in a community tend to remain constant regardless of the disaster. The alternative is the proliferation of individual plans which repeatedly set the same resources against similar problems. The all hazards approach also, by definition, covers previously unknown and unexpected disasters which could cause confusion in a disaster-specific planning process. In most countries the only exception to the all hazards approach is specific planning for certain hazardous sites, such as chemical processing and storage facilities, where the location, type and potential magnitude of possible disasters are predictable.

Comprehensive Emergency Management

Emergency planning is typically perceived as a two-stage process involving the survey of hazards and resources and the preparation of plans to cope with any potential disaster. In the United States, however, emergency planning has been expanded to achieve its maximum potential and has been redefined in a broad framework as a four-stage, cyclical, continuous process which is described as comprehensive emergency management (CEM).[4] It is the view of the author that such an approach should be the eventual aim of every national emergency planning process. The four phases of CEM are described as mitigation, preparedness, response and recovery.

Mitigation can take place either during recovery from a past disaster or as part of the preparation for potential future disasters. Mitigation includes all actions taken to eliminate or reduce the degree of long-term risk to human life and property from natural and technological hazards.

Preparedness is undertaken before a disaster occurs and includes the preparation of emergency operational plans, the assembly of necessary supplies and equipment, the training of response personnel and the exercising of emergency plans and systems.

Response takes place immediately before, during and directly after a disaster and includes warning, search and rescue, emergency medical assistance and other emergency assistance to the public.

Recovery is generally regarded as occurring in two sections, immediate recovery and long-term recovery. Immediate recovery activities include damage assessment, clearing of debris and restoration of essential supplies and services. Long-term recovery activities include ongoing assistance to victims, reconstruction of damaged buildings and services and the mitigation process.

Legislation

Because emergency planning is at the same time a complex administrative process and a vital component in the effort to protect and safeguard citizens, many governments have resorted to legislation to promote their aims in this area. Not surprisingly the legislative process in most countries has tended to be most active in the aftermath of disaster incidents. Legislation typically involves some or all of the following issues: a statutory requirement on local authorities to engage in emergency planning, including requirements for the holding of exercises; the setting up of national emergency planning authorities, with responsibility for the promotion of emergency planning; and funding arrangements for ongoing emergency planning and post-disaster relief and reconstruction.

The Dutch Disaster Act of 1985 obliges all local authorities to draw up disaster plans.[5] Furthermore it requires each local authority to create a special operational plan, including a decision-making scenario, for all possible calamities that might occur on specific disaster-prone sites, such as chemical plants, within their area of responsibility. This latter requirement, which has not proved feasible in practice, indicates the intention of the Dutch government to force detailed emergency planning on local authorities. The Spanish Law on Civil Protection of 1985 gives authority to the General Directorate for Civil Protection, the national organisation for emergency planning, to create regulations for the preparation of emergency plans at all administrative levels within the state.[6]

The Canadian Emergency Preparedness Act of 1988

created Emergency Preparedness Canada (EPC) as an
autonomous branch of the Canadian public service.[7] EPC
was charged with the advancement of civil preparedness in
Canada for emergencies of all types as well as facilitating
and co-ordinating the development and implementation of
civil emergency plans. The British Civil Protection in
Peacetime Act of 1986 gave legal status to the *de facto*
situation which had developed in Britain by empowering
local authorities to use their civil defence resources to
respond to peacetime civil emergencies. The United States
has over the years introduced extensive disaster legislation
including the Disaster Relief Act of 1974 which authorises
the President to declare an emergency or major disaster in
an affected area and permits the use of federal resources to
help local response and recovery.

National Emergency Planning Organisations

Many governments have created national organisations to
promote and organise effective emergency planning. These
organisations can be located within government departments or alternatively can be autonomous bodies. In Britain
emergency planning is organised by the Emergency Services
Division of the Home Office. However, the alarming
succession of disasters that occurred in Britain in the late
1980s caused the Home Secretary to create a new post of
Civil Emergencies Advisor in November 1989. This move
may well be seen eventually as the first step towards the
creation of an autonomous civil emergency organisation in
Britain.

In Canada EPC is involved in co-ordinating federal
emergency policies, sponsoring research on emergency
preparedness, exercising and evaluating crisis management
plans, developing and delivering training programmes,
liaising with local emergency planning groups and
maintaining an emergency co-ordination centre to monitor
and report on emergencies throughout Canada. The annual
budget of EPC is of the order of nineteen million Canadian
dollars.[8] The largest national emergency planning
organisation in the world is the Federal Emergency
Management Agency of the United States (FEMA), which
has a staffing level of 2,300 and is involved in similar
activities to its Canadian counterpart.[9]

Training

Emergency planning is widely regarded as a skill which is imparted by education and training and developed by means of exercises. To this end a number of countries have developed emergency planning colleges and training centres. In the United States FEMA's National Emergency Training Centre at Emmetsburg, Maryland, provides training for approximately 4,000 emergency planning professionals while simultaneously providing correspondence courses in emergency planning to 70,000 participants each year.[10] These correspondence courses are an integral part of FEMA's policy of providing extensive information to the public on emergency planning. In Canada the Emergency Preparedness College in Ontario provides training in emergency planning for 3,000 public officials each year.[11] In Britain training is provided at the former Civil Defence College at Easingwold, now known as the Emergency Planning College. Furthermore, in a new and interesting development, Hatfield Polytechnic has announced the launch of Britain's first postgraduate course on emergency management – a year-long full-time course leading to an MSc in Civil Emergency Management.[12]

European Community

A recent international initiative of particular interest in the context of this study is the development of the Civil Protection Programme of the European Community. This programme has been promoted as part of the drive towards a 'People's Europe'. The objective of the programme, which was adopted by the Council of Ministers in May 1987, is the development of a Community-wide strategy that would involve the use of all available Community resources in the fight against disasters. The programme is intended to be comprehensive and as such will not be confined to the *response* to disasters. Rather, in a manner reminiscent of the approach of the United States, the programme is envisaged as promoting activity in the four areas of forecasting, prevention, disaster management and reconstruction. To help in the achievement of these aims the Community has allocated a 'modest' budget for civil protection.

To date action under the programme has included the

sponsoring of research at a number of centres, the holding of international exercises, the establishment of a permanent network of liaison posts in each member country and the compilation of a manual on civil protection within the Community.[13] This manual describes the current legislative and organisational basis for emergency planning in each of the twelve countries of the Community. From this document it appears that Ireland is the only member state in which there is no legislative basis for emergency planning.

—4—

Emergency Planning in Ireland

Background

It would appear that emergency planning has never been awarded a high priority in Ireland. This is understandable in light of the absence of most of the major disaster threats which have traditionally promoted emergency planning in other countries. Ireland's geographic position has saved it from all of the major natural disaster agents such as earthquakes, volcanoes, tornadoes and avalanches. The country does occasionally experience severe storms, floods and blizzards, but serious loss of life is not usual during such events. In relative terms Ireland is not heavily industrialised and therefore the threat of industrial accidents and the volumes of hazardous materials in transit or storage are low by the standards of many neighbouring countries. Ireland's small and generally quite dispersed population means that the commuter transport accidents which result from high concentrations of population are unusual. The population, moreover, lives in areas which, almost without exception, have been inhabited for centuries and therefore the problems caused by modern human settlements on flood plains and other such hazardous areas, which are particularly common in the United States, do not arise.

The Republic of Ireland remained neutral during the Cold War and therefore the threat of nuclear attack was never perceived as particularly serious. It was of course recognised that a nuclear attack on the United Kingdom would have serious consequences for Ireland and a Civil Defence Force was formed in 1951 to assist the population in the aftermath of such an event. However, not surprisingly, the resources committed to civil defence were small by comparison with those countries which were deeply

involved in the Cold War. This low level of resource investment was also a function of Ireland's economic position.
Ireland has been and remains a poor country relative to
most other developed countries and therefore resources
have never been available for civil defence or emergency
planning at the levels which are common in countries such
as the United States and United Kingdom.

Major Accident Plans

The history of emergency planning in Ireland has, until
now, been largely undocumented. However, it would appear
that the first attempts at emergency planning were undertaken by the Southern Health Board during 1973. The first
plan, known as a major accident plan, was produced by that
board in 1974 and subsequently all eight health boards
produced major accident plans. These plans established
procedures for declaring emergencies and also detailed co-
ordinating procedures for the different emergency service
organisations which would be involved in a major accident,
including the Gardaí and the fire brigades. In substance the
plans were largely concerned with the rescue of victims and
their transfer to hospitals.

On 1 August 1980 a rail disaster occurred at Buttevant,
County Cork, in which seventeen people were killed and
forty-one injured. In December of that year the Department
of Health convened a conference on major accident plans
in Dublin to which representatives of the eight health
boards were invited and at which the response to the
Buttevant disaster was discussed. The purpose of the
conference was to facilitate the boards in an examination of
their major accident plans, in the context of the Buttevant
incident, so that all plans could be updated in light of the
experience gained. In his opening address to the
conference the Minister for Health stated, *inter alia*, that
'the Health Boards are expected to play the primary role in
preparing plans for Major Accidents'.[1]

In April 1981 the Department of Health issued a circular
to all health boards containing guidelines for the major
accident plans.[2] These guidelines were quite extensive and
covered the different roles of health boards, local
authorities, Gardaí and the army, as well as voluntary groups
such as the Red Cross. The guidelines envisaged major

accident plans which would include an alert phase and in which the plan could be activated at three different levels, depending on the severity of the incident involved. The guidelines provided details on numerous issues such as mobilisation procedures, the organisation of the incident site, arrangements for temporary mortuaries and arrangements for the provision of information to relatives and the media.

Department of the Environment Initiative

On 8 May 1981 the Minister for the Environment issued a circular to all local authorities requesting that they prepare emergency plans in accordance with a separate set of guidelines which had been prepared by his department.[3] These guidelines provided a planning framework for local authorities in the preparation of their emergency plans and of necessity involved many issues already covered in the Department of Health document. However it would appear that there had been no consultation between the two departments while the documents were being prepared and Department of Health officials appear to have been taken by surprise by the issue of the Department of the Environment document. This situation may be explained by the suggestion that the Department of the Environment was under considerable pressure at that time in the aftermath of the Stardust disaster, which had occurred earlier in the year.

At health board level the response to the Department of the Environment initiative would appear to have been a mixture of surprise and resentment. Problems appear to have been caused in particular by the recommendation that each local authority should designate an official who would assume the role of 'controller of operations' at the incident site. Since the functions of the controller were not clearly defined, health board officials were concerned that this represented a unilateral attempt by the local authorities to assume control of all personnel at the scene of a major emergency and this was, of course, unacceptable.

Further difficulties were created by differing definitions of the types of events which would trigger the implementation of the plans. The major accident plans of the health boards were designed to deal with incidents involving high numbers of casualties and at that time twenty or more

seriously injured was taken as a guide. The proposed major
emergency plans of the local authorities, on the other hand,
were concerned with a wide range of events including those
with no casualty element, such as blizzards and major
pollution incidents. In terms of co-ordination, the health
boards were concerned that the eight major accident plans
which covered the entire country were to be augmented by
thirty-one local authority plans with a resulting tendency
towards confusion and duplication.

It is clear that at the time the spirit of co-operation, which
is so necessary for effective interorganisational emergency
planning, was at a very low ebb. In December 1981 officials
of the Departments of the Environment and Health met
with health board chief executives. The various contentious
issues were discussed, including the issue of the controller
of operations, but no resolution of the differing views
appears to have been achieved. Following severe blizzards
which closed many roads early in 1982, the Department of
the Taoiseach became involved in the process and convened
an Inter Departmental Committee on Emergency Planning.
This committee included representatives from the Departments of the Environment, Justice, Health and Defence
under the chairmanship of a representative from the Department of the Taoiseach.

Major Emergency Planning Initiative

In December 1982 this committee issued a draft document
setting out a framework for co-ordinated planning for major
emergencies[4] and sought observations on this document
from all relevant agencies including local authorities, health
boards and the Gardaí. The committee considered the
matter for two years and examined all observations received.
During this period it would appear that, while the Department of the Taoiseach remained in the chair, the Department
of the Environment gradually assumed a leading role in the
committee. The significance of this development was that it
confirmed the Department of the Environment as the lead
government department in emergency planning and represented a resolution of the conflict, which had arisen in
1981, in favour of that department and the local authorities.
There are indications that this 'victory' is still resented in
some health board circles.

In February 1985 the Department of the Environment issued a 'major emergency planning package' to all local authorities which included the final version of the framework document,[5] a model emergency plan for local authorities,[6] an explanatory memorandum on the model plan[7] and a document giving general advice and guidelines.[8] At the same time each local authority was requested to review and update its emergency plans in the light of these documents. Copies of the package were forwarded by the Department of Health to each health board with a request that each should update its emergency plans having regard to the framework document. It is presumed that the Department of Justice took similar action in relation to the Gardaí.

The major emergency planning package contained much excellent material. The incidents which would trigger the activation of the plan were designated as major emergencies and the planning process was to be known as major emergency planning. A major emergency was defined as:

> . . . any event which, usually with little or no warning, causes or threatens:
> – death or injury
> – serious disruption of essential services or
> – damage to property
> beyond the normal capabilities of the Gardaí, Local Authorities (including Fire Authorities) and Health Services.

As well as defining major emergencies the framework document also specified a number of other critical issues. The area of operation of each plan was described. Procedures which allowed the plan to be activated by any one of the three emergency services were detailed. The main functions and principal duties of each of the services were described. Three positions, to be known as 'controller of operations', were created at the site of the emergency, one for each of the services. Apart from incidents during which there was a potential danger to the emergency services, when the fire service would have overall control of the 'danger area', the three controllers were each to control, direct and co-ordinate the activities of their own agency's services only.

Co-ordinating Group

The framework document also introduced the concept of a co-ordinating group which was to consist of the city/county manager, chief executive officer of the health board and chief superintendent of the Gardaí or alternates nominated by them. Following activation of the major emergency plan any member could call the group together at a designated group headquarters. The functions of the co-ordinating group during an emergency response were listed as the monitoring of the activities of all agencies responding to the emergency, maintaining liaison between the agencies, arranging for the mobilisation of additional resources as required, giving directions and policy decisions as required, and facilitating the distribution of information to the media and the general public.

The framework document made it clear that the major emergency plan, in action, was to consist of the activated, combined plans of the three different agencies, which had been defined and co-ordinated in advance. This was a strange and unusual concept and resulted more, perhaps, from a need for compromise within the committee than any recognised emergency planning theory. For example no cognisance appears to have been taken of the obvious conflict between this concept and the need for secrecy on the part of the Gardaí in relation to their plans. Responsibility for ensuring that all plans were co-ordinated was given to the co-ordinating group and the task of convening the co-ordinating group for that purpose was allocated to the local city/county manager. Despite this central role allocated to the co-ordinating groups in the major emergency planning process it would appear that, in large measure, these groups have never been activated.

The failure to activate the co-ordinating groups has, of course, had serious consequences for the effective implementation of the entire major emergency package. The author has seen no document referring to or explaining this failure but it is possible that the following factors may be at least partly responsible. The designated members of the co-ordinating groups include the chief executive officers of large public organisations whose work-load in the past five to ten years has been significantly increased by cutbacks in public expenditure. In this situation the work of the co-ordinating groups, for which there is no statutory requirement, no public pressure and no financial support, must obviously rate a very low priority.

A further disincentive is the unrealistic configuration of many co-ordinating groups. In the Mid-West region, for example, the framework document suggested four co-ordinating groups, with one each in Counties Clare, Tipperary (NR) and Limerick and one in Limerick City. The chief executive officer of the Mid-Western Health Board was designated as a member of each group. In terms of emergency planning this arrangement was not really practical as, for example, any major emergency in the Limerick City area would inevitably involve the surrounding county councils in the response. It is possible that the Dublin base of the committee which produced the framework document may explain this oversight.

It is the view of the author that the concept of a co-ordinating group of chief executive officers as a high-level body charged with responsibility for emergency planning carried out in a particular area has merit. However the role assigned to these groups in a disaster situation is not at all practical. In most organisations the chief executive is the natural leader of the crisis management team and as such is required within the organisation in times of crisis. Furthermore the suggestion that the manager/chief executive should be absent from the organisation at a time of crisis would, if implemented, create extra communication problems for the emergency service organisations as each attempted to maintain contact with its chief executive in the co-ordinating group headquarters.

Site-Based Response

This issue is symptomatic of the general approach of the framework document and model plan which are very much concerned with a site-based response to disasters. This approach is founded on the common misconception of disasters as larger versions of normal emergencies, which Tierney and Quarantelli described as basically flawed. Furthermore it reflects a failure to understand the major off-site organisational management issues which are critical to good emergency planning.

One result of this flaw in the framework documentation is that many local authorities and health boards have concentrated much of their attention on the operational services such as the fire service and the ambulance service. However in any disaster situation it is likely that these services will perform well since their disaster role is similar to their everyday role. Organisation and interorganisation management, on the other hand, are much more likely to be sources of difficulty in the aftermath of any disaster.

Framework

The major emergency framework document was based on the all hazards approach and was particularly strong on establishing responsibilities. In contrast to the earlier health board major accident plans the proposed major emergency plans were to include no provision for an alert and only one level of response. This represented a serious reduction in flexibility which is particularly significant in certain situations such as threatened aircraft accidents where it may be desirable to declare an alert.

The documents made it clear that the planning process is a continuous one including an assessment of local hazards and resources, preparation of a response plan, appraisal and testing of the plan by means of exercises, and modification of the plan as required in a reiterative cyclical manner. Detailed guidelines were provided on the assessment of local hazards and of the community's ability to respond to each specific threat. The importance of exercises was stressed and a schedule of exercises was outlined involving progressively more complex formats.

The co-ordinating group was charged with responsibility for organising exercises which would test the ability of all the emergency services under disaster conditions, and in the light of experience gained at these exercises to review each individual service plan as necessary. The need for specialised training in the context of emergency planning was noted and particular attention was drawn to the training needs of information officers.

When the major emergency planning package was issued in 1985 it was followed by a series of regional seminars which were intended to brief those involved in the planning process at local level. However no legislation on major

emergency planning was ever introduced and to date all
activity on major emergency planning has been undertaken
in accordance with department circular letters only. No extra
resources were made available to the health boards or local
authorities to help fund research, training, exercises or any
other part of the planning process. Apart from the seminars
there appears to have been little input by the committee or
the relevant government departments into the planning
process at local level. The only form of monitoring appears
to have consisted of a request to each local organisation that
a completed plan be submitted to the relevant department.
The committee was in fact disbanded within a short period
of the launch of the package.

Implementation

Against this background the local authorities set about the
task of preparing major emergency plans in 1985 and most
of the plans were completed during 1986. In general the
plans contained extensive lists of contact persons, both
within the local authorities and in outside organisations,
whose assistance or resources might be required in the
event of an emergency. Given the small size of most urban
areas outside of Dublin and the limited specialist resources
available in most regions it is not surprising that the
different plans include extensive duplication. In reality
many of these plans were little more than replicas of the
model plan with the requisite local names inserted.

Discussions which the author has had with officials in a
number of areas indicate that, in general, comprehensive
hazard analyses were not carried out and that the co-
ordinating groups were not involved in the preparation of
the plans. Thus two critical elements of the planning process
as envisioned by the Inter Departmental Committee appear
to have been ignored.

Exercises were held in a number of areas with differing
levels of success. Generally the exercises exposed significant
problems and deficiencies, which is of course part of the
purpose of exercises. However it is the apparent absence of
any follow up on the exercises, in the form of alterations to
plans and the conducting of further exercises to check on
the amended plans, which is a cause for concern here.

Review

A new Inter Departmental Committee with representatives from the Departments of the Environment, Health, Justice and Defence was established by the government in 1986. This committee was asked to advise on and monitor all peacetime emergency planning arrangements. The committee considered the package that had been issued by the previous committee as well as feedback on actual emergencies and exercises which had tested the major emergency plans. In a report dated February 1989 the committee expressed the view that 'the guidance documentation on Emergency Planning is adequate to prepare local emergency response plans'.[9]

Thereafter the report refers obliquely to certain problem areas. It mentions, *inter alia*, confusion at local level, in some instances, as to whether or not the plan should be activated; the essential part of major hazard identification in emergency planning; the fact that consideration might be given to the need for some training of designated information officers; the importance of good com-munications between responding organisations; and the importance of having the plans tested. In the area of com-munications with the public the report states that 'it is not clear that all emergency services have given sufficient thought to the arrangements that need to be made to keep the public (and the media, as appropriate) informed of developments relating to a major emergency'. There is no reference to the failure to activate the co-ordinating groups.

Committee on Public Safety and Crowd Control

Following the Hillsborough Football Ground disaster in April 1989 and the subsequent Taylor report, the Irish government established a high-level committee under the chairmanship of the Hon Mr Justice Liam Hamilton to examine all aspects of public safety and crowd control at major public events, with particular reference to sporting events, music festivals and concerts. This committee examined arrangements for major games and race meetings as well as major outdoor and indoor concerts and other such events, visiting venues all over Ireland, in London and in Spain. In light of the fact that Ireland has never experienced a disaster at such an event the prominence and resources awarded to this investigation, relative to the review of emergency planning, is surprising. The committee report illustrates certain gaps in the legislation in this area and recommends extra powers for the Gardaí.[10] It also recommends that a national authority for safety at sports grounds should be established and a formal code of practice for safety at sports grounds should be prepared by that authority; this code, furthermore, should be given legal standing by the enactment of legislation.

The committee considered emergency planning but does not appear to have investigated the actual status of the process, noting in passing that 'provision is made for the heads of the local emergency services to meet annually to ensure the individual plans are co-ordinated and any areas of conflict are resolved'. However the committee did express concern at the generic character of the major emergency plans and recommended that a separate emergency plan should be prepared for each major sports ground. To facilitate this process the report includes a model emergency plan for Croke Park which was prepared by a sub-committee. This plan gives detailed instructions to designated members of the Garda Síochána both at the site and in the Garda Headquarters at Harcourt Square, designates areas for specific purposes such as mortuaries, includes procedures for two different scenarios and provides a map of the Croke Park area with exits and emergency service routes shown.

IPA Seminars

At the request of the local authorities the Institute of Public Administration organised a series of workshops on emergency planning during May and June 1990. No representatives from health boards or the Gardaí were invited to attend. A synopsis of the proceedings of these workshops indicated concern among local authority personnel at a perceived lack of communication and co-ordination with the other emergency bodies at local and regional level as well as uncertainty as to the precise roles of different specialists at the site of major incidents.[11] The need for training of key personnel in a number of areas, including the carrying out of hazard analysis, was recognised.

The advantage of regular exercises was mentioned, including the possibility of organising desk top and field exercises on alternate years. Of particular interest, however, are the significant number of issues listed as remaining to be resolved. These include the identity, role, authority and accountability of the controller of operations; the availability of key personnel outside office hours; a series of communications issues such as the need for an integrated system; the provision of training for controllers; the funding of training; and the role, location, membership and power of the co-ordinating group.

This extensive list of outstanding issues is a serious indictment of the major emergency planning initiative and includes a number of items which have been a cause of considerable controversy and discussion within local authorities for a number of years. One such issue relates to the relationship between the chief fire officer and the county engineer in the event of a disaster. The local authority plans generally nominate the county engineer as controller of operations except in those cases where a 'danger area' is involved, when the chief fire officer is nominated as controller of operations. This ambiguity has, in the past, led to a certain degree of concern among chief fire officers. This matter is further confused by the issue of 'on call' arrangements and payments. The major emergency plans of the local authorities specify that the controller of operations will take control of local authority services at the scene of a major emergency. However the nominated controllers work a normal five-day week and no provision has ever been made for them to be 'on call' outside of working hours. This issue has been the subject of protracted negotiations and as yet no final resolution has been achieved. A similar situation exists in the health boards.

Survey of Practice

Since the practice of emergency planning in many areas appeared to differ significantly from that which was described in the original documentation, a survey was conducted by the author, during June and July 1991, of the emergency planning process in five organisations. This survey took the form of a structured interview with a key official in each of four local authorities and a health board, with questions on each of the following areas: status of major emergency planning within the organisation, co-operation between organisations, preparation of the written plan, content of the plan, training and exercises.

Status of Emergency Planning Within the Organisation

All of the organisations had engaged in emergency planning, mainly as a result of the requests from the relevant department that they should do so, although there appeared to be a growing realisation of the need for such planning. The goals of planning were seen mainly as the specification of tasks and preparation for a co-ordinated response. There appeared to be some ambiguity as to the location of responsibility for emergency planning within the organisations – different interviewees nominated chief executives, city/county engineers and fire officers.

Emergency planning was not practised as a continuous process. No organisation had an emergency planning budget. No resource or hazard analysis appeared to have been carried out, although several organisations had listed the major hazardous facilities within their areas of jurisdiction.

Co-operation Between Organisations

None of the interviewees believed that the manager or chief executive of their organisation had been involved in a co-ordination group meeting during the previous year, apart from two who met during an exercise. None of the plans included an agreed location for co-ordinating group meetings. All of the organisations had informal arrangements for the sharing of resources with neighbouring organisations and some had formal arrangements for the sharing of some resources.

Preparation of the Written Plan

Several of the plans were written in 1986, with a five-year projected life to review, and therefore new plans had been or were being prepared during 1991. One organisation updated its plan each year and did not intend to conduct any major review. All of the plans were written on the basis of the framework document, with no special training for those who prepared the plans and no special research. Only one organisation consulted outside organisations during the preparation of the plan although most organisations examined other plans.

Content of the Plan

All of the plans identified key personnel and some identified replacements. However, apart from the co-ordinating groups, which were expected to play a liaison role, none of the plans included off-site management arrangements. While in general they specified the responsibilities of key personnel, only one plan included any instructions. It would appear that the plans were not fully correlated, included no role for the media, and were not communicated to the public. Furthermore they included no arrangements for organising volunteers at the site of a major incident; for staff rotation in the event of a lengthy incident; or for post-incident trauma counselling of emergency workers. All plans appeared to have been submitted to the relevant government depart-ments but there was no evidence that they were approved or otherwise commented upon. None of the plans included special arrangements for the rapid approval of necessary spending although all interviewees indicated that this would not be a problem.

Training

Only one organisation had engaged in emergency planning related training during the previous year. This training was directed at personnel at operator level and no management training was carried out.

Exercises

One of the five organisations had never taken part in any exercise. One organisation had never taken part in an exercise involving other organisations, although it had conducted its own table top exercises. One organisation organised an interorganisational exercise some years ago but apart from that had never taken part in any other exercise. One organisation had never conducted an exercise but had taken part in a number of interorganisational exercises, organised by others. Only one organisation had itself conducted an exercise and taken part in inter-organisational exercises organised by others. Each inter-organisational exercise mentioned appeared to have been organised by a single organisation. In general the responses would indicate that most exercises were less than satisfactory and that there was much dissatisfaction with the results. Much comment centred on the preparations made by some of the participating organisations for pre-arranged exercises, which tended to exacerbate interservice rivalry and mis-understanding. None of the plans had been altered in any way as a result of experience gained during exercises.

Conclusion

The results of this limited survey cannot, of course, be automatically regarded as representative of the entire country. However, following discussions with officials involved in emergency planning throughout the country, the author is convinced that, with some notable exceptions, the survey accurately reflected the status of emergency planning in most areas.

The major emergency planning initiative has, therefore, succeeded in creating an awareness of emergency planning in local organisations as well as achieving agreement on the major roles of the different organisations. However the concept of a nationwide series of co-ordinated plans, prepared by an interorganisational co-ordinating group, on the basis of local hazard and resource analysis, which would be exercised and tested at regular intervals, appears to be quite some distance from the reality. In that situation it is obvious that a comprehensive review of emergency planning is now overdue.

—5—

Evaluation and Recommendations

Analysis of Emergency Planning in Ireland

Positive Factors

Any analysis of emergency planning in Ireland must take into account certain underlying factors which make Ireland different from many of the developed countries of Europe and North America. Ireland is a small country with a low population density. As a result most Irish organisations are small by international standards and thus many officials, with no direct work-related contact, are known to one another through social contact in clubs, professional organisations, etc. Furthermore, Irish business is generally conducted without excessive formality and as a result relationships are established earlier than in more formal societies. Finally, state officials and the public share one language and thus a major obstacle to communication which occurs in areas such as Canada, Belgium and southern California is avoided. These factors combine to create a climate in which co-operation within organisations and between organisations can be achieved quickly, when required, without the necessity for formalised systems such as the mutual assistance contracts that are common among emergency organisations in countries like the United States.

It should also be noted that local authorities and health boards are already engaged in many activities which can be regarded as part of a comprehensive-type emergency planning process. These activities include the planning process by which strict controls are imposed on all new developments, particularly places of public assembly and industrial facilities. The long-drawn-out planning appeals procedures which are now a common feature of any new chemical industry development bear testimony to the rigorous manner in which such facilities are examined before any construction commences. Under the Fire Services Act of 1981 local fire authorities are allocated powers and responsibilities in relation to a wide range of premises to which the public has access or which present special risks. Under this Act fire authority inspectors have the power to carry out inspections of premises and, in the case of any which are considered to be potentially dangerous, fire notices can be served forbidding the use of the premises for certain purposes or requiring that action be taken to make the premises safe. These procedures can be regarded as an integral part of disaster mitigation.

Furthermore much of the ongoing development of the fire and ambulance services is a significant part of disaster preparedness. For example, recent progress in the development of computer-aided mobilisation for the fire service can be regarded as a major advance.[1] This development, which has been piloted in the Mid-West region, includes the preparation of an address database that includes every townland, colloquial placename, village and town in the region as well as a record of all special risk premises such as factories and hospitals. The severity of likely incidents for each special risk premises has been assessed and a predetermined attendance to deal with such incidents has been calculated and recorded. A resource database of all fire appliances in the region is also included as well as a map model indicating the relative locations of all fire stations, special risk premises and named location. The system can offer the officer on duty the optimum list of appliances to deal with any particular incident and an extensive communication network facilitates the transfer of detailed information concerning the site to appliances on their way to an incident. However, to date the system has not been shared with the other emergency services.

Possible Disasters

Against these positive factors must be placed the funda-mental paradox that in most areas of human activity it is the persons and organisations which are least at risk that tend to be least prepared and therefore suffer most when things go wrong. This paradox can be illustrated by an examination of the relative positions of Ireland and Britain in the context of disasters. There is a similar pattern of natural disasters in both countries but Britain is more heavily populated and more industrialised and therefore disasters are more likely to occur there. However, if a disaster does occur, there are substantially more resources available in Britain at local and national level to help with the response. Thus emergency planning, which seeks to bridge the gap between potential disasters and available resources, is relatively more important in Ireland than in Britain, unless of course Ireland is regarded as being free of potential disasters.

It appears highly unlikely that Ireland will ever be subject to major natural disasters, such as earthquakes and volcanoes, which are a constant threat in other areas of the world. There are, however, a number of potential disasters whose occurrence in Ireland cannot be ruled out and these can be grouped under five main headings as follows: aircraft crashes, other transport accidents, dangerous substance incidents, major crowd incidents and miscellaneous incidents.

Aircraft crashes: A safety analysis prepared by the Boeing Aircraft Manufacturing Group has indicated that the number of commercial aircraft crashes worldwide is likely to increase to twenty per annum by the year 2005, compared to an average of fifteen per annum during the 1980s.[2] This fore-casted increase is linked directly to a projected increase in the volume of world passenger traffic. Irish air traffic is a small component of the world's total, but the Boeing study indicated that transatlantic traffic represents approximately 15 per cent of world air traffic. Since more than 60 per cent of this traffic crosses Irish air space, the possibility of an aircraft crash in Ireland sometime in the future cannot be discounted.[3] The regular diversion of aircraft 'in difficulties' to Shannon and the two crashes that occurred close to Ireland in the recent past, that is Pan Am and Air India, strongly reinforce this argument.

Other traffic accidents: The serious incidents which occurred in Ireland during the past twenty years involved a significant number of bus and train accidents, including two major train crashes at Buttevant and Cherryville. Looking ahead there are certain trends which tend to underpin the likeli-hood of more such accidents in the future. Poor quality roads contribute to traffic accidents, not only directly, but also indirectly through the damage caused to vehicles. The poor state of Irish roads has been highlighted on numerous occasions and the continuing difficulties with local authority financing would suggest that the road system will tend to deteriorate rather than improve in the near future. On another front the ongoing financial difficulties of CIE will tend to depress maintenance spending, reduce safety standards and thus create vulnerabilities. Similar developments at British Rail would appear to have been a major contributor to the train crash at Clapham Junction. There are strong indications therefore that serious traffic accidents are likely to continue in the future.

Dangerous substance incidents: During the past twenty years the use of toxic materials in Irish industry and agriculture has increased dramatically. The same period has seen the widespread introduction of LPG as a fuel in vehicles, homes and industry. Consequently, large quantities of dangerous materials are stored and transported throughout the country. The safety record of the Irish chemical industry and Irish fuel companies is generally good but accidents can and do occur in most areas of human activity. Unfortunately an initially minor accident involving dangerous materials can quickly escalate into a disaster. This was graphically illustrated in 1986 when a fire in the Sandoz warehouse in Basle, where pesticides were stored, produced clouds of dangerous gases and the water used to fight the fire severely polluted the Rhine. The occurrence of a similar event in Ireland cannot be ruled out.

Major crowd incidents: The behaviour of Irish crowds at sporting and social events is in the main exemplary. However any situation in which large numbers of people are congregated in confined spaces contains inherent vulnerabilities. Much improvement in this area has resulted from the introduction of stricter building controls following the Stardust disaster. However it is not difficult to visualise several possible scenarios which could lead to tragedy wherever large crowds are gathered. For example, a fire in a mobile fast food outlet, spreading to other outlets parked alongside and with resulting gas cylinder explosions, would have a devastating effect in a crowded street as crowds assembled or departed from any one of the numerous major sporting and social events which take place in Ireland each year. The possibility of such an event is recognised in the concerns expressed in the report of the Committee on Public Safety and Crowd Control.

Miscellaneous incidents: The future is of course unpredictable and there are also other areas which may give rise to future disasters. These include the possibility of an accidental emission from a British nuclear installation, terrorist actions resulting from the conflict in Northern Ireland, more severe storms and flooding than have been customary resulting from global climatic changes, or mass food poisoning incidents resulting from the increased industrialisation of the human food chain. This latter danger was graphically illustrated by the Jalisco tragedy in 1985 when thirty people died in southern California having eaten contaminated cheese.[4] Finally there is the possibility of the unknown, the disaster whose cause and effects are not yet known but which could arise with fearful consequences.

It is not within the scope of this study to prepare a statistical analysis of all possible disaster agents and associated risk factors, and thereby attempt to predict the probability and size of future Irish disasters. However Ireland clearly cannot be regarded as immune from disasters, and given the relatively low level of resources to deal with any disasters which do occur, the case for effective emergency planning is all the more evident.

Model of National Emergency Planning Process

If Ireland is to have effective nationwide emergency planning then a government strategy is required so that appropriate emergency planning will be undertaken at local level throughout the country. Any successful strategy must involve a comprehensive, continuous planning process: this study proposes a model for a national emergency planning process, which is illustrated in Figure 4, to facilitate the achievement of such a result. The process involves five distinct phases as follows: 1) establish aims and objectives; 2) produce a national planning framework; 3) promote emergency planning at local level; 4) provide guidance and training; 5) monitor results; as well as a series of iterative correcting procedures.

Figure 4: Model of national emergency planning process

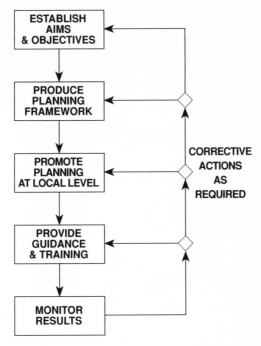

Phase 1 – Establish Aims and Objectives

Emergency planning is a variable process which can be practised at many different levels, from the very basic, involving merely the specification of persons and roles in times of disaster, to the highly sophisticated, involving large, permanent emergency planning departments, extensive training and numerous exercises. During Phase 1 it is necessary for the government to establish the required level of emergency planning, based on the estimated relationship between perceived hazards and the resources in place to meet them, in the context of the finances available for emergency planning. Having established aims in this area, quantifiable objectives are required so that progress can be monitored. Typical objectives might include the establishment of certain internal and interorganisational structures, the training of specified percentages of relevant staff and the holding of certain exercises. To be meaningful all objectives must be assigned an appropriate timeframe.

Phase 2 – Produce National Planning Framework

The national planning framework includes all important decisions on the methods by which the objectives of emergency planning are to be achieved. The matters for decision are wide-ranging and include such items as which government department, if any, and which local organisations will be responsible for emergency planning, what is the optimum format for the emergency plans, how is emergency planning to be promoted in local organisations, what type of training is to be provided for local emergency planners, who are the key officials at local level and how is the national planning process to be monitored.

Phase 3 – Promote Emergency Planning at Local Level

Having decided on a national planning framework it is necessary to promote the framework to local organisations and to the key personnel within those organisations. Promotion can take a number of different forms including seminars to introduce the concept, circular letters requesting that local organisations engage in emergency planning or statutory instruments insisting on same. The level of promotion required is a matter of judgement.

Phase 4 – Provide Guidance and Training

Emergency planning is a complex activity and like many other complex activities it is not possible to become proficient merely by reading a manual. Training and guidance, therefore, must be made available to local emergency planners. A number of different training strategies are possible but it would seem obvious that initially an intensive course would be required to produce a cadre of trained emergency planners who would help achieve the required first movement in emergency planning. Such a development would be in keeping with international trends which have witnessed the establishment of national emergency planning colleges in, for instance, the US, the UK and Canada.

Phase 5 – Monitor Results

In all areas of human activity where new skills are introduced, monitoring of the results is common so as to ensure that the skills have been successfully transferred. Monitoring is a reiterative process involving, usually, a continuous improvement until the required levels have been achieved. Monitoring of emergency planning, the effects of which are somewhat subjective, will always be difficult. However, if the initial objectives of the process are adequately specified these can act as useful reference points for the monitoring process. Monitoring is further complicated by the strong possibility that antagonisms may be raised at local level by the monitoring process. In part this resentment is unavoidable but could be greatly reduced by drawing monitors from the cadre of trained local emergency planners referred to earlier. Without monitoring it is not possible to ascertain if the planning process is achieving its aims and monitoring also facilitates the introduction of any necessary corrections.

Correcting Procedures

The model of the national emergency planning process has four iterative correcting loops. At the lowest level inadequacies in the planning process which can be ascribed to local misinterpretation can be corrected by additional guidance or training as required. If problems persist, despite guidance and training, then corrective actions at progressively higher levels may be required. The monitoring process may reveal that local organisations are not allocating sufficient time and resources to the process and a change in the promotional mix may be required. For instance, it may be necessary for the government to provide extra resources or to introduce a statutory requirement for emergency planning by local organisations.

Monitoring the emergency planning process will in time reveal areas of the national planning framework which require modification. A thorough review of the framework should be carried out at pre-set intervals, perhaps every ten years, with flexibility on the time-scale if the necessity for change at an earlier stage becomes apparent. Finally it may be necessary to review the aims and objectives of the entire process, particularly if it transpires that it is not possible to achieve the prescribed objectives within the available budget.

The entire process as described above involves considerable inputs over a significant period by both government and local organisations. It would seem wise therefore to consider a pilot project at the framework planning stage so that any inconsistencies or inadequacies may be identified. This approach is commonly used by the Department of Education when new education schemes are introduced and in the case of a complex process like emergency planning could have significant benefits.

Examination of Major Emergency Planning Initiative

When the existing major emergency planning initiative is examined in the light of the model national emergency planning process, the underlying causes of many of the present problems become apparent. There is no direct evidence as to the procedures followed during the initiation of the process, that is, Phase 1. However it is possible to speculate that a major aim was the resolution of the confused situation which had arisen between the health boards and local authorities without incurring any major expenditure. During Phase 2 a reasonable plan format was produced although there were some deficiencies, as has already been illustrated. However the decisions on promotion, training and monitoring, taken either directly or by default, are open to serious questioning.

During Phase 3 emergency planning was promoted by means of seminars as well as circular letters instructing relevant local organisations to prepare emergency plans. Phase 4, training and guidance, does not appear to have featured at all during the initiative. The monitoring process, Phase 5, appears to have consisted of requests that each local organisation submit its completed plan to the relevant department, visits by department officials to some exercises and the endeavours of the review committee. None of these activities appears to have been successful in providing feedback to local planners where this was required or in causing alterations to those aspects of the national process which were not successful.

Proposal for a New Initiative

Given the present state of emergency planning it is evident that a fresh initiative is required. This initiative must involve a thorough review of each phase of the emergency planning process, the production of a new national emergency planning framework and ongoing guidance and monitoring of emergency planning throughout the state. One of the first issues that must be addressed is the present division of responsibility for emergency planning at government level which can be seen as a fundamental cause of many of the existing problems. Responsibility must be allocated to one department and a strong argument can be made for the nomination of the Department of Justice. However the history of emergency planning in Ireland would indicate that it would perhaps be wise to choose the Department of the Environment since that department has been the 'lead' department for several years now.

National Authority for Emergency Planning

To facilitate the introduction and execution of a comprehensive national process the author would recommend the establishment of a national authority for emergency planning similar to the national authority for Safety at sports grounds recommended by the Committee on Public Safety and Crowd Control, which met for the first time in August 1991.

The proposed national authority would be broadly based with technical and non-technical personnel including representatives from the three key government departments, the Gardaí, local authority management, the fire service, health board management, the ambulance service and one of the voluntary bodies involved in disaster response such as the Red Cross. The authority would be responsible for the preparation of a national emergency planning framework, the monitoring of the operation of the framework and the furnishing of an annual report on emergency planning to the relevant minister.

On appointment the authority would survey the actual position of emergency planning at local level throughout the country and thereafter conduct a thorough re-examination of the national emergency planning process. It is the contention of this study that such an operation should result in a programme along the following lines.

Phase 1 – Establish Aims and Objectives

Given the observed levels of hazards and resources, the present state of emergency planning, and the level of resources likely to be available for emergency planning in the foreseeable future, a moderate level of emergency planning would appear to be a reasonable aim in Ireland. Typical objectives of the planning process might be that all relevant local organisations would undertake a basic emergency planning process, that groups of local organisations would engage in effective co-ordination of their planning processes, and that each group of organisations would be capable of conducting an effective full-scale inter-organisational exercise within a period of five years.

Phase 2 – Produce National Planning Framework

The national planning framework required to achieve these objectives would need extensive consideration and consultation at government level, but one possible format is suggested here. In March 1991 a Cabinet sub-committee proposed new structures for local government involving a new tier at regional level.[5] The proposal involves the creation of eight regional authorities whose areas of control co-incide in large measure with the areas of operation of the eight existing health boards. This development presents a unique opportunity to place emergency planning on a regional basis, which is more in keeping with the likely response to any real disaster.

In each region an emergency management committee should be formed comprising the managers of each of the local authorities, the chief executive of the health board and the chief superintendents of the Garda divisions. This management committee should meet at least once a year and, most importantly, should form a working group of nominated emergency planning officers to carry on the process of emergency planning throughout the year. This working group would have one member from each of the organisations involved and would report at least once each year to the management committee. The duties of the working group would be to organise emergency planning at regional level, to ensure that the individual plans of each organisation were co-ordinated with the regional or sub-regional plan and to act as a liaison group between the organisations.

Initially the working group would conduct a regional hazard analysis, listing all known hazards within the region and assessing the potential disaster effect of each. This hazard analysis should be a comprehensive, proactive process and thus the group should be encouraged to make recommendations on any mitigation which might be feasible. Typical mitigation recommendations might include special arrangements for major sporting and social events or additional safety precautions in chemical plants.

The working group would conduct a detailed resource analysis, listing all available relevant resources within the region or, in the case of resources not available locally, the nearest available source. Such a list would include people with particular skills, such as doctors and translators, and equipment and facilities both in public service organisations and in the private sector. This process could involve extensive enquiries with private and semi-state companies and ultimately negotiation with such interests on the arrangements whereby necessary resources could be made available if required. For example, detailed discussions with Telecom Éireann, on a regional basis, could involve issues such as the provision of extra telephone lines to emergency organisations and the reservation of a significant section of the Eircell network for emergency communication during a disaster situation. Similar discussions could involve arrangements for the provision of reconnaissance and/or rescue helicopters by the Air Corps and Irish Helicopters. In the case of certain limited items which the group believed were necessary and which did not appear to be readily available locally, collective purchase and central storage might be recommended so that the items would be available if required. The resulting resource database would be eminently suitable for storage on a minicomputer. This form of storage facilitates regular updating of the information and speedy distribution to the participating organisations by means of floppy disks or eventually by electronic data interchange (EDI).

A useful adjunct to such a database would be a list of names and addresses of those who would be particularly at risk in a disaster situation, such as the handicapped, the elderly and other vulnerable groups. This list could be used to direct special assistance to such persons in many disaster situations, particularly if it became necessary to evacuate an area because of flooding, poisonous vapour clouds or other such hazards.

Figure 5: Regional plan format

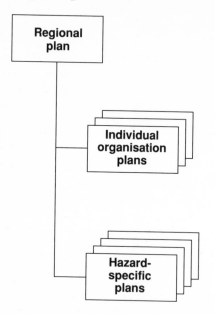

The working group would also prepare a basic regional plan or a series of sub-regional plans where the geography of the region was not conducive to one single plan. The format of these plans would be similar to that illustrated in Figure 5. These plans would be similar in many ways to the existing major emergency plans and would include details such as the area of operation, the procedures for activation and the major duties and responsibilities of the responding organisations. The plans would include a number of possible levels of activation, typically involving an alert level, a local level where the response is confined and a regional or sub-regional level where all possible resources are required.

In place of the co-ordinating group the proposed national planning framework would place responsibility for local emergency planning with the regional management committee and through it with the working group. In a disaster situation the working group, or alternates nominated by its members, would act as the main liaison between local organisations.

Each organisation would devise its own operational plans and these would be considered as appendices to the main plan, although not physically attached to it. The working group would prepare specific hazard plans which would also be regarded as appendices to the main plan. These specific hazard plans would be few in number and would be concerned with certain hazards which the group regarded as deserving of special attention. These would typically include airports and any facility where major quantities of hazardous substances were stored. The major stadia emergency plans proposed by the Committee on Public Safety and Crowd Control and the off-site procedures required by the Seveso Directive of the European Community[6] would be included among such plans. Each specific hazard plan would pre-set certain procedures such as designated assembly areas and temporary mortuary sites in the case of airports and major stadia, and public warnings, decontamination arrangements and evacuation procedures in the case of hazardous substance facilities.

Emergency planning committees would be formed within individual organisations. These would include the organisation's representative on the regional working group, the chief executive officer, the designated information officer and other relevant managers of administrative and operational divisions. This committee would be responsible for organising the preparation of a series of internal operational plans which together would form that organisation's portion of the regional emergency plan. This committee or a sub-committee of it would typically be designated as the crisis management team.

Within the local authorities the operational plans would include a mobilisation plan, fire brigade plan, crisis management team plan, civil defence plan, public evacuation plan, emergency shelter plan, emergency feeding plan, major pollution incident plan, media plan and an outline recovery plan. Health board operational plans would include a mobilisation plan, ambulance plan, crisis management team plan, operational plans for each hospital, mass poisoning plan, hospital evacuation plan, post traumatic stress counselling plan, media plan and a community welfare plan. The Garda operational plans would include a mobilisation plan, traffic control plan, site security plan, casualty bureau plan, temporary mortuary plan, victim identification plan, public information plan, terrorist incident plan and dignitary security plan.

Some of these operational plans are already, at least in

part, in existence in each of the services. The preparation and subsequent availability of many of the other plans could be of ongoing benefit to the organisations involved apart from their potential disaster role. In particular the existence of a designated crisis management team and a crisis management plan could be of immense benefit to all of the organisations involved under specific circumstances. A graphic illustration of this point was provided by a recent incident in which the 'wrong' babies were given to two mothers in an Irish maternity hospital. The resulting crisis, with intense international media interest and difficult decision making under stressful conditions, involved some of the attributes of a disaster situation. The existence of a trained crisis management team would have been of considerable benefit in that situation.

Phase 3 – Promote Emergency Planning at Local Level

Decisions on the method of promotion of the national emergency planning process at local level must involve detailed consideration of three elements: funding, responsibilities and powers. Funding will always be a sensitive matter. However an agreement that central government would fund the cost of emergency planning at local level would act as a strong incentive.

Responsibility for emergency planning must be established clearly at local level. The existing package which divided responsibility and included promotion by means of circular letters has obviously not succeeded in all areas. Serious consideration must be given, therefore, to the issue of ministerial orders requiring relevant local organisations to engage in comprehensive emergency planning, to nominate emergency planning officers and to exercise and review plans at regular intervals.

When specific hazards are examined at local level it is likely that special powers will be required to compel compliance with some mitigation requirements. For example the Committee on Public Safety and Crowd Control drew attention to the absence of any legislative powers for the Gardaí to enforce safety precautions at major crowd events. The committee recommended that legislation be introduced in this area as a matter of urgency and it would appear expedient to include these powers in a comprehensive Emergency Planning Act which would allocate finance and responsibility to designated organisations and provide the powers necessary to allow these duties to be executed effectively.

Phase 4 – Provide Guidance and Training

Guidance and training must play an important role in the implementation of the national emergency planning programme. Guidance must be provided by the national authority to ensure that the stated procedures are understood, any ambiguities are explained and the programme is implemented in a uniform fashion throughout the country. Training must be regarded as a continuous process involving, firstly, the technical members of the national authority, and later, members of the regional working groups, members of crisis management teams and relevant staff at all levels within the local organisations. Initial training would require the invitation of foreign emergency planning specialists to lecture in Ireland or the despatch of a small group abroad for training. Eventually, however, it should be possible to have most training carried out by Irish specialists.

At local level the regional working groups would be central to the training process. Initial training of the members of the working groups should help to establish a reservoir of knowledge of emergency planning in each region. Building on that foundation, training courses could be organised on a regional basis for all relevant staff with consequential economies of scale and improved co-ordination. Within each organisation training of staff at all levels would be undertaken on a phased basis with particular attention being devoted to the training of management.

Any examination of emergency planning training must include a review of the role of the Civil Defence school. This school, located in Dublin's Phoenix Park, is under the control of the Department of Defence and at present appears to have no role to play in emergency planning. Control of the college should pass to the department with responsibility for emergency planning and the college should be orientated from civil defence towards emergency planning.

Phase 5 – Monitor Results

Exercises are an integral part of emergency planning but
they also provide an ongoing opportunity to monitor the
effectiveness of the entire process. Internal organisational
exercises would be conducted in each organisation
beginning with modest exercises involving each service
separately and expanding to include all services within the
organisation. At interorganisational level exercises would be
organised by the regional working group and initially these
would be of a basic nature, probably involving desk top
scenarios only. However the aim would be to move to
exercises of escalating complexity with a view to achieving
the objective of a full-scale interorganisational exercise
within five years.

The existence of eight regional working groups on
emergency planning would in time create a set of experts,
with specialists in specific areas, who would be available to
provide advice, training and guidance to individual
organisations. The working groups could also supply
monitors for individual organisation exercises or interorganisational exercises. These monitors would have
enhanced credibility because of their experience and thus
should help to reduce hostility to the monitoring process.

Correcting Procedures

The iterative nature of the monitoring phase has already
been described and with trained emergency planners at
regional level the difficulties at local level should be
minimal. This should simplify the role of the national
authority and allow it to concentrate its review of the
process on any necessary changes in the national framework
and the level of promotion.

Ultimately it is the government which must decide on the
aims and objectives of emergency planning. Changes may
be required if it is found not to be possible to reach the set
objectives within the budget provided or if it becomes
obvious that the objectives themselves are inadequate. The
latter possibility is unfortunately most likely to occur in the
aftermath of a tragedy.

The primary costs involved in the implementation of the
national process, such as the costs of training, are relatively

small. Any computation of the secondary costs, related to extra duties for existing public officials, is highly subjective and is beyond the scope of this study. However it is the author's view that emergency planning is a low-cost preventative measure and the government which ignores emergency planning does so at its peril. In this regard the final sentence of the recommendations of the Stardust Tribunal has a salutary message. Referring to the fire services which had been underfunded for many years prior to that tragedy, the report states:

> . . . it is clear that their continuing neglect in Ireland has now contributed to a disaster on an appalling scale which will cast a shadow across one Dublin community for years, and perhaps generations, to come.[7]

Is it necessary that the report of the next disaster tribunal should end with an expression of similar sentiments concerning emergency planning before action is taken?

Conclusion

Emergency planning is a complex process involving predictions about the future, preparation for events which are of indeterminate type, location and frequency, and co-operation between groups and organisations which are often in competition for scarce resources. Outside of disaster occasions there is no demand from the public for emergency planning and as a result it does not rate highly, if at all, on the political agenda. Thus there are many reasons why officials, with busy schedules and a multitude of demands, would tend to procrastinate in the area of emergency planning.

Emergency planning, however, is a low-cost precautionary process which can yield tremendous dividends. Timely action can prevent the occurrence of some disasters. Speedy, efficient and effective mobilisation and use of all available resources can greatly reduce human suffering and distress during a disaster as well as substantially reduce the cost of the disaster response, both in the short and long term. The value and necessity of emergency planning have been recognised by the many governments throughout the developed world that have invested significant resources in the process.

In Ireland the absence of major natural disaster threats has resulted in a very low priority for emergency planning. However a number of inherent advantages mean that an effective emergency planning process could be created in Ireland without large expenditure. The major emergency planning initiative has succeeded in alerting many organisations to the need for emergency planning. Furthermore it has created a framework within which the emergency services can be mobilised during a disaster and in which the overall roles of the different services have been defined.

However the initiative has not achieved its full potential for a number of reasons. Promotion and training were minimal and there appears to have been no effective monitoring of the results. Many of the plans prepared under the initiative are 'paper plans' only and much of the process, as detailed in the initiative documentation, has never been implemented.

During the next disaster individuals may emerge who, by their initiative, leadership and courage may cause everything to be 'all right on the night'. On the other hand the disaster response may be hit by 'Murphy's Law', in which case the omissions listed above may be comprehensively exposed during the response and at the subsequent tribunal. Should such a situation arise charges of negligence may well be difficult to dispute and the minor costs involved in establishing a reasonable level of emergency planning throughout the country will appear paltry indeed, compared even to the costs of the tribunal itself.

In the present situation the managers of local authorities, Garda chief superintendents and the chief executives of the health boards appear to be in a particularly invidious position. The major emergency planning initiative documents placed upon them responsibility for the preparation of major emergency plans and the co-ordination of those plans at local level by means of the co-ordinating groups. The fact that the co-ordinating groups appear never to have been mobilised to execute any of this work could be held to be a major contributory factor to any future, less than successful, disaster response.

In this situation it is recommended that the co-ordinating groups should meet as soon as possible, preferably on a regional basis, and establish working sub-groups to begin the process of hazard analysis, resource analysis, plan co-ordination, etc. At the same time both individually and through their national associations they should communicate to the government the shortcomings of the existing major emergency planning framework and the urgent need for resources, further powers and training.

In the author's opinion the government should immediately establish a high-level, independent committee, preferably under the chairmanship of a High Court judge, to examine all aspects of emergency planning in Ireland. On the presumption that the findings of such a committee would be similar to the findings of this study, the author would recommend the establishment of a national authority for emergency planning and at the same time an examination of the aims of emergency planning so that the national authority can be charged with the achievement of set objectives within a specific timeframe.

The most important of the factors that will determine the future of emergency planning in Ireland is the level of government commitment to the process. At present it would appear that this commitment is sadly lacking and the state of the public finances may be used as a reason for the postponement of any new initiative. However the person who must eventually explain to a disaster tribunal why no ministerial attention or significant resources were made available for the emergency planning process over many years may very much regret such a decision.

Appendix 1

List of incidents in the Republic of Ireland from 1972 to 1990 compiled from information collected by Captain B. Phelan of the Southern Health Board

1972	Dublin	Bomb	29 hurt
1972	Dublin	Bombs	2 dead, 126 hurt
1974	Dublin	Bombs	1 dead, 14 hurt
1974	Monaghan	Bombs	5 dead, 20 hurt
1975	Gorey	Train crash	5 dead, 30 hurt
1976	Castlebar	Bus crash	47 hurt
1976	Cork	Ship/gas explosion	2 dead
1977	Roscommon	Rail crossing accident	4 dead
1977	Shannon	Aircraft take-off crash	50 hurt
1978	Borrisoleigh	Bus crash	1 dead, 40 hurt
1978	Glounthane	Bus crash	5 dead, 27 hurt
1979	Bantry	Oil tanker explosion	50 dead
1979	Fastnet	Storm/yacht race	15 dead, 64 hurt
1979	Arklow	Train crash	22 hurt
1979	Dalkey	Train crash	36 hurt
1980	Clare	Bus crash	3 dead, 32 hurt
1980	Buttevant	Train crash	17 dead, 41 hurt
1981	Whitegate	Oil tank explosion	1 dead
1981	Stardust	Fire	46 dead, 104 hurt
1982	Meath	Bus crash	34 hurt
1983	Cherryville	Train crash	7 dead, 25 hurt
1983	Tipperary	Truck/chemical leak DiPhenylMethaneDiisoCynate	
1984	Killiney	Building collapse	1 dead, 4 hurt
1984	Gort	Bus crash	15 hurt
1984	Cork	Grain silo dust explosion	2 dead
1985	Charleville	Train/ammonia leak	
1985	Slane	Bus crash	26 hurt
1985	Dunboyne	Light aircraft crash	6 hurt
1985	Athlone	Train/chemical leak Methyl Acrylate	
1985	Off SW coast	Air India aircraft crash	329 dead
1986	Douglas, Cork	Swimming pool gas leak	25 hurt
1987	Ballsbridge	Building/gas explosion	2 dead

1987	Curragh	Bus/truck crash	16 hurt
1987	Naas	Bus/car crash	2 dead, 1 hurt
1987	Ballyneety	Bus crash	1 dead, 49 hurt
1987	Clogheen	Aircraft crash	4 dead
1987	Galway	Bus crash	1 dead, 6 hurt
1988	Dublin	Potassium cyanide leak	29 hurt
1989	Clare	Bus/car crash	1 dead, 16 hurt
1989	Clondalkin	DiMethylCyclo HexylAmine leak	9 hurt
1989	Claremorris	Train crash	70 hurt
1989	Dublin	Bus overturn	14 hurt
1990	Inchicore	Phenyl sulphonate spill	40 hurt

Appendix 2

List of incidents in the United Kingdom from 1960 to 1990 compiled from information collected by the University of Bradford Disaster Planning and Limitation Unit

1960	Glasgow	Whisky bond store fire	19 dead
1965	North Sea	Oil rig capsized	13 dead
1966	Barmouth	Pleasure boat accident	15 dead
1966	Cornwall	Motor cruiser sank	31 dead
1966	Aberfan	Coal waste tip slide	147 dead
1967	Hither Green	Derailment of train	49 dead
1968	Glasgow	Warehouse fire	22 dead
1969	Gatwick	Boeing 727 crash	50 dead
1971	Ibrox Pk	Crush of spectators	66 dead
1971	Clarkston	Gas explosion	20 dead
1972	Staines	Trident aircraft crash	118 dead
1973	Isle of Man	Leisure centre fire	50 dead
1974	M62	Bomb explosion in coach	12 dead
1974	Flixborough	Explosion of cyclohexane	28 dead
1974	Birmingham	Bomb explosions in pubs	21 dead
1975	London	Underground train crash	42 dead
1975	Scunthorpe	Blast furnace explosion	11 dead
1977	Hessle	Fire in old people's home	11 dead
1978	Belfast	Bomb in restaurant	20 dead
1978	Taunton	Fire on a train	12 dead
1979	Manchester	Fire in Woolworths store	12 dead
1979	Sumburgh	Hawker aircraft crash	17 dead
1979	Warrenpoint	Bomb explosion	18 dead
1980	Soho	Fire in drinking club	37 dead
1981	Norfolk	Helicopter crash	13 dead
1981	Penlee	Lifeboat wrecked	16 dead
1982	Ballykelly	Bomb explosion	17 dead
1983	Scilly Is.	Helicopter crash	20 dead
1983	Stornoway	Aircraft crashed	10 dead
1984	Abbeystead	Explosion in valve house	16 dead
1984	Polmont	Train crash	13 dead
1984	Uttoxeter	Vickers aircraft crash	11 dead
1984	M25 motorway	Multiple crash in fog	10 dead
1985	S-fordshire	Legionnaires' disease	30 dead
1985	Bradford	Football stadium fire	56 dead

1985	Manchester	Fire on Boeing 737	55 dead
1986	M4 motorway	Van crossed barrier	13 dead
1986	Sumbugh	Helicopter crash	45 dead
1987	Zeebrugge	Ferry capsized	193 dead
1987	Hungerford	Gunman attack	17 dead
1987	S. England	Hurricane and storms	20 dead
1987	M61 motorway	Tanker collision	13 dead
1987	Enniskillen	Bomb explosion	11 dead
1987	King's Cross	Underground station fire	31 dead
1988	Piper Alpha	Explosion/oil platform	167 dead
1988	Clapham	Multiple train crash	35 dead
1988	Lockerbie	Pan Am 747 exploded	270 dead
1989	Kegworth	737 crashed onto M1	47 dead
1989	Hillsborough	Crush of spectators	95 dead
1989	Thames	Boat sank	51 dead
1989	Deal	Bomb explosion	11 dead
1990	West Country	Gales and floods	45 dead

Appendix 3

List of incidents in the European Community from 1950 to 1990 compiled from information collected by the European Commission

1951	Italy	Flooding of River Po	
1952	England	London smog	12,000 dead
1953	Greece	Earthquake on islands	455 dead, 4,400 hurt
1953	Holland	Costal storms & flooding	2,000 dead
1953	Belgium	Costal storms & flooding	
1953	England	Costal storms & flooding	
1954	Greece	Earthquake	25 dead, 157 hurt
1954	Germany	Flooding in Bavaria	
1956	Greece	Earthquake	53 dead, 100 hurt
1956	Belgium	Mining disaster	262 dead
1959	Spain	Dam burst	144 dead
1959	France	Dam burst	421 dead
1960	Holland	Aircraft crash	7 dead
1961	Holland	Chemical accident	95 dead
1962	Italy	Earthquake	16 dead, 200 hurt
1962	Spain	Flooding in Barcelona	500 dead
1962	Germany	Coastal storms & flooding	400 dead
1963	Italy	Landslide and flooding	2,118 dead
1965	Holland	Explosion on tanker	16 dead
1966	Portugal	Forest fire	21 dead
1966	Italy	Flooding in Florence	
1967	Portugal	Flooding in Lisbon	500 dead
1967	Belgium	Fire in Brussels	325 dead
1968	Italy	Earthquake in Sicily	800 dead
1968	Holland	Chemical factory fire	
1970	Italy	Flooding of River Po	
1970	France	Avalanches	120 dead
1971	Holland	Chemical fire	9 dead, 2 hurt
1971	Holland	Hotel fire in Eindhoven	11 dead, 12 hurt
1971	Holland	Hospital fire	13 dead
1972	Holland	Road accident	13 dead, 30 hurt
1973	Spain	Flooding	350 dead
1975	Germany	Forest fire	
1975	Holland	Chemical explosion	14 dead, 109 hurt

1976	England	Chemical explosion (Flixboro)	28 dead
1976	Italy	Earthquakes	1,200 dead
1976	Italy	Chemical accident (Seveso)	
1976	Holland	Chemical accident	24 dead
1976	Holland	Forest fire at Arnhem	
1978	Spain	Gas tanker explosion	216 dead
1978	Greece	Earthquake	45 dead, 220 hurt
1979	Ireland	Oil tanker explosion	50 dead
1979	Italy	Earthquake	4,500 dead
1980	Portugal	Earthquake	56 dead, 500 hurt
1981	Greece	Earthquake	19 dead, 500 hurt
1981	Ireland	Fire in disco (Stardust)	48 dead, 214 hurt
1981	Holland	Aircraft crash	17 dead
1983	Belgium	Earthquake	1 dead, 26 hurt
1983	Portugal	Flooding in Lisbon	7 dead
1984	Italy	Earthquake	
1985	Belgium	Heysel stadium riot	38 dead, 400 hurt
1985	Spain	Oil tanker explosion	32 dead
1985	Italy	Dam burst	289 dead
1985	Portugal	Forest fires	14 dead
1985	England	Bradford stadium fire	50 dead
1986	Portugal	Forest fire	13 dead
1986	Greece	Earthquake	20 dead, 300 hurt
1986	Italy	Landslides	146 dead
1987	Belgium	Ferry capsized	189 dead
1987	Italy	Flooding	53 dead
1987	Greece	Heat wave	1,500 dead
1987	England	Severe storms	21 dead
1987	France	Flooding in Bornand	11 dead
1987	France	Severe storms in Brittany	11 dead
1988	France	Flooding	11 dead
1988	Portugal	Fire in Lisbon	
1989	Italy	Forest fire in Sardinia	18 dead
1989	Portugal	Aircraft crash	145 dead
1989	Portugal	River flooding	
1990	Italy	Earthquake in Sicily	12 dead, 99 hurt
1990	Portugal	Marine pollution	
1990	Belgium	Severe storms	19 dead

Notes to Chapters

Introduction

1. Dumfries and Galloway Regional Council, *Lockerbie: A Local Authority Response to the Disaster* (Dumfries, 1989).
2. Kartez, J.D., 'Emergency Planning: An Adaptive Approach', *Baseline Data Report*, Volume 20, No. 5, 1988.

Chapter 1: Development of Emergency Planning

1. Emergency Preparedness Canada, *Emergency Planning for Federal Departments* (Ottawa, 1989).
2. Keller, A.Z., 'The Bradford Disaster Scale', paper delivered to the First Disaster Prevention and Limitation Conference at the University of Bradford, September 1989.
3. Commission of the European Communities, *Towards a European Society: Civil Protection* (Brussels, 1988).
4. London Emergency Planning Information Centre, *Acts of God? An Investigation into Disasters* (London, 1990).
5. Whittow, J.B., 'Earthquakes and Building Design: An Overview', *Disaster Management*, Volume 2, No. 2, 1989.
6. Tierney, K. and Quarantelli, E.L., 'Needed Innovation in the Delivery of Emergency Medical Services in Disasters: Present and Future', *Disaster Management*, Volume 2, No. 2, 1989.
7. Western, K.A., 'The Epidemiology of Natural and Man-made Disasters – The Present State of the Art', Dissertation submitted for the Academic Diploma in Tropical Public Health, University of London (1972).
8. Keller, A.Z., Wilson, H. and Kara-Zaitri, C., 'The Bradford Disaster Scale', *Disaster Management*, Volume 2, No. 4, 1990.

9. Horlick-Jones, T. and Peters, G., 'Measuring Disaster Trends Part 1: Some Observations on the Bradford Scale', *Disaster Management*, Volume 3, No. 3, 1991.
10. Stahel, W.R., 'Interdependence of Factors in Disasters', paper delivered to the Second Disaster Prevention and Limitation Conference at the University of Bradford, September 1990.
11. London Emergency Planning Information Centre, *op. cit.*
12. Foster, H.F., *Disaster Planning* (New York, 1980).
13. Mitroff, I., 'Crises Management: Cutting Through the Confusion', *Sloan Management Review*, Winter 1988.

Chapter 2: Literature Review

1. Hodgkinson, P.E., 'The Zeebrugge Disaster: Psycho-Social Care in the U.K.', *Disaster Management*, Volume 2, No. 3, 1990; Grollmes, E.B., 'Air Disaster Response: The Psychological, the Other Disaster', *Disaster Management*, Volume 3, No. 3, 1991.
2. Duckworth, E.H., 'Disaster Work and Psychological Trauma', *Disaster Management*, Volume 1, No. 2, 1988.
3. Jenkins, J., 'It's The Doers Wot Get The Blame', *Sunday Times*, 20 August 1989.
4. Hart, P. and Pijnenburg, B., 'Patterns of Crisis Decision Making: The Heizel Stadium Tragedy', Proceedings of Conference on Crisis Management at the Catholic University of Mons, Belgium, 1987.
5. *Report of the Tribunal ⸴ Enquiry on Disaster at Whiddy Island, Bantry, Co. Cork* (Dublin, 1980).
6. *Report of the Tribunal of Enquiry on the Fire at the Stardust, Artane, Dublin on the 14th February 1981* (Dublin, 1982).
7. Southern Health Board, *Air India Disaster: Implementation of Major Accident Plan* (Cork, 1985).
8. Fayol, H., *General and Industrial Management* (London, 1949).
9. Richardson, B. and Richardson, R., *Business Planning, An Approach to Strategic Management* (London, 1989).
10. Warren, E.K., *Long Range Planning: The Executive Viewpoint* (1966).
11. Mitroff, I., *op. cit.*
12. Fink, S., *Crises Management, Planning for the Inevitable* (New York, 1986).

13. Weick, K.E., 'Organisational Culture as a Source of High Reliability', *California Management Review*, Volume 29, No. 2, Winter 1987.
14. Nelkin, N., 'Risk Reporting and the Management of Industrial Crises', *Journal of Management Studies*, Volume 25, No. 4, July 1988.
15. Scanlon, T.J., 'The Role of the Media in Crisis Situations', Proceedings of Conference on Crisis Management at the Catholic University of Mons, Belgium, 1987.
16. Fink, S., *op. cit.*
17. Comfort, L.K., 'Planning and Legislation for Crisis Situations', Proceedings of Conference on Crisis Management at the Catholic University of Mons, Belgium, 1987.
18. Rosenthal, U., 'Crisis Management: An Unusual Approach', Proceedings of Conference on Crisis Management at the Catholic University of Mons, Belgium, 1987.
19. Quarantelli, E.L., 'Education – The Cost Effective Counter Disaster Measure', paper delivered at Emergency 84 Conference.
20. Mileti, D.S. and Sorensen, J.H., 'The Determinants of Organisational Effectiveness in Responding to Low Probability Catastrophic Events', *The Columbia Journal of World Business*, Volume 22, No. 1, Spring 1987.
21. Quarantelli, E.L., 'Disaster Crisis Management: A Summary of Research Findings', *Journal of Management Studies*, Volume 25, No. 4, July 1988.
22. Quarantelli, E.L., 'Education'.

Chapter 3: International Perspective

1. Comfort, L.K., *op. cit.*
2. *Emergency Planning Guidance to Local Authorities*, Home Office (London, 1991).
3. House of Commons Reply by Mr J. Patten, Secretary of State for the Home Department, quoted in *Civil Protection*, Issue No. 16, Autumn 1990.
4. *The C.E.O.'s Disaster Survival Kit*, Federal Emergency Management Agency (Washington, October 1988).
5. Van Duin, M.J. and Rosenthal, U., 'Disaster Planning in the Greater Rotterdam Area: Laws, Scenarios and Exercises', *Disaster Management*, Volume 2, No. 2, 1989.

6. Lazuen, J.S. and Rutz Del Arbol, E., 'Fundamental Standards for the Planning and Management of Emergencies of Chemical Origin', paper delivered to the European Conference on Emergency Planning for Industrial Hazards, Varese, Italy, November 1987.
7. EPC, *Report to Parliament on the Operation of the Emergency Preparedness Act: April 1989-March 1990* (Ottawa, 1989).
8. *Ibid.*
9. FEMA, *This is the Federal Emergency Management Agency* (Washington, September 1990).
10. *Ibid.*
11. EPC, *Report to Parliament.*
12. Hatfield Polytechnic Prospectus (May 1991).
13. *Vade-mecum de la Protection Civile dans la Communauté Européenne*, Commission des Communautés Européennes (Brussels, December 1990).

Chapter 4: Emergency Planning in Ireland

1. Woods, Dr M., Minister for Health, Address to Conference on Major Accident Plans in the Custom House, Dublin on 12 December 1980.
2. 'Guidelines to Health Boards Regarding Plans to Cope with Major Accidents', Department of Health, Dublin, April 1981.
3. 'Planning for Major Emergencies', Department of the Environment, Dublin, May 1981.
4. 'Emergency Planning: Draft Framework for Co-ordinated Response to Major Emergency', Dublin, December 1982.
5. 'Emergency Planning: Framework for Co-ordinated Response to Major Emergency', Dublin, November 1984.
6. 'Local Authority Major Emergency Plan, Model', Issue No. 1, Department of the Environment.
7. 'Explanatory Memorandum on the Model Local Authority Major Emergency Plan', Department of the Environment, Dublin, February 1985.
8. 'Emergency Planning, General Advice and Guidelines', Department of the Environment, Dublin, February 1985.
9. *Report of the Inter Departmental Committee on Peacetime Emergency Planning*, Dublin, February 1989.

10. *Report of Committee on Public Safety and Crowd Control*, Dublin, February 1990.
11. O'Keeffe, A. and O'Hea, M., 'Emergency Planning: Synopsis of Series of Workshops held May/June 1990', Institute of Public Administration, Dublin 1990.

Chapter 5: Evaluation and Recommendations

1. Tobin, R. and Lomas, R.A., 'The use of GIS in the Irish Computer-aided Mobilisation Project for the Fire Service', paper presented to the Annual Conference of the Chief Fire Officers Association, Ennis, May 1991.
2. 'Statistical Analysis Suggests Rise in Airliner Accident Rate', *International Civil Aviation Organisation Journal*, October 1990.
3. Information supplied to the author by the Department of Tourism and Transport.
4. Fink, S., *op. cit.*
5. 'Local Government Reform', press release issued by the Department of the Environment, Dublin, 7 March 1991.
6. Commission of the European Communities, Council Directive 82/501/EEC on the Major Accident Hazards of Certain Industrial Activities (the 'Seveso' Directive), 24 June 1982.
7. *Report of Tribunal of Enquiry.*

Select Bibliography

Commission of the European Communities, *Towards a European Society: Civil Protection* (Brussels, 1988).

Dumfries and Galloway Regional Council, *Lockerbie: A Local Authority Response to the Disaster* (Dumfries, 1989).

Federal Emergency Management Agency, *The C.E.O.'s Disaster Survival Kit* (Washington, October 1988).

Fink, S., *Crises Management: Planning for the Inevitable* (New York, 1986).

Foster, H.F., *Disaster Planning* (New York, 1980).

Horlick-Jones, T. and Peters, G., 'Measuring Disaster Trends Part 1: Some Observations on the Bradford Scale', *Disaster Management*, Volume 3, No. 3, 1991.

Kartez, J.D., 'Emergency Planning: An Adaptive Approach', *Baseline Data Report*, Volume 20, No. 5, 1988.

Keller, A.Z., Wilson, H. and Kara-Zaitri, C., 'The Bradford Disaster Scale', *Disaster Management*, Volume 2, No. 4, 1990.

Mileti, D.S. and Sorensen, J.H., 'The Determinants of Organisational Effectiveness in Responding to Low Probability Catastrophic Events', *The Columbia Journal of World Business*, Volume 22, No. 1, Spring 1987.

Mitroff, I., 'Crises Management: Cutting Through the Confusion', *Sloan Management Review*, Winter 1988.

Proceedings of European Conference on Emergency Planning for Industrial Hazards, Varese, Italy, November 1987.

Quarantelli, E.L., 'Disaster Crisis Management: A Summary of Research Findings', *Journal of Management Studies*, Volume 25, No. 4, July 1988.

Rosenthal, U. (ed.), *Crisis Management: An International Perspective*, Proceedings of Conference on Crisis Management at the Catholic University of Mons, Belgium, 1987.

London Emergency Planning Information Centre, *Acts of God? An Investigation into Disasters* (London, 1990).

Tierney, K. and Quarantelli, E.L., 'Needed Innovation in the Delivery of Emergency Medical Services in Disasters: Present and Future', *Disaster Management*, Volume 2, No. 2, 1989.